NLP for Traders and Investors

Personal strategies to give you the edge over those using just fundamental and technical analysis

Terry Carroll

TTL

TTL is an imprint of
Take That Ltd.
P.O.Box 200
Harrogate
HG1 2YR
ENGLAND

email:sales@takethat.co.uk

www.takethat.co.uk/books.htm

TTL are always keen to receive ideas and manuscripts for new financial books. Please send details to the address above.

TTL books are available at special quantity discounts to use as premiums and sales promotions. For more information, please contact the Director of Special Sales at the above address or contact your local bookshop.

ISBN 1-873668-81-3

Contents

Introduction

"At least 70 per cent of day traders lose money" (*North American Securities Administrators Association, August 1999*).

In July 1999, Mark Barton, a 'day-trader' who had made heavy losses on the stock market, 'went on a killing spree in Atlanta'. After killing his family, he opened fire in both the offices where he had conducted his trading.

We may never know exactly why this happened, although some of us have known the fear of losing everything. Most of us also know the feeling of great success from some moment in our lives, however brief. When things have gone wrong, however, how often have we run the movie of that previous success? How many of us could run negative patterns in our minds with ease? Did we ever criticise ourselves, or 'beat ourselves up' inside, if things didn't work out?

How did we do that? Where and how did we learn to faultlessly follow the same negative patterns or strategies in our language, or our lives? If we have the capacity to have learned once how to run such exquisite behaviours, without missing a step; if we could understand precisely the mechanics of how to construct and programme such behaviours into ourselves, then there is no limit to what we can do with positive patterns.

I have had an interest in the stock market since I first went to university in 1967 to read business studies. Then, in 1972, my father asked me to invest some of his capital. Within a year, I lost all of the money. This was a shock to my confidence and self-belief. He was very good about it and I resolved to learn from experience. Reviewing my errors of judgement, I decided that the best strategy for any speculation was to work on the basis of minimising losses rather than maximising profits.

Three years later he asked me to use my analytical skills to work out a system for horse racing. Based totally on statistical analysis of the data available in the newspapers, I turned his starting capital of 10 units into 125 units in a matter of weeks. Exhausted by the four hours of preparation every day, I returned the money to a grateful parent.

Among the lessons I learned from these experiences were:

- The importance of proper research and preparation;
- The need for balance in investment decisions; and
- The value of rational judgement in determining strategies and when to buy or sell, rather than being driven by fear of loss or even failure.

You may be able to identify with these experiences. Betting on hunches or riding the tide of emotion can be exciting ways to play the market when you have capital to lose. If you are *gambling* your savings or core capital, especially where other stakeholders (including one's family) are involved, this can be a distressing, frightening or highly stressful experience as losses mount.

How can we change our behaviour and/or find the necessary personal resources to create the positive patterns we desire? While this book will not, in itself, make you money, through understanding and personal change it can help to create the patterns for rational trading untainted by fear, thereby reducing your chance of loss and optimising the possibility of success. It may also change other aspects of your life.

If you were to go forward to a time when you had understood yourself and your behaviours, had minimised or eliminated the negatives and accentuated or developed new positive patterns, how does that possibility feel inside you now?

NLP - the still new art and science of being and getting what you want

In 1972, in California, Richard Bandler and John Grinder began the study of excellence in human language and behaviour. They listened to, observed and felt the behaviours of three great therapists - Milton Erickson, Fritz Perls and Virginia Satir (each a giant in their own field). They analysed and disaggregated the patterns of language and behaviour and then set about modelling them, to create tools and techniques for anyone to understand, resolve and change their own behaviours at will.

Now, 28 years on, NLP Practitioner is the fastest growing profession in the West. People are transforming their own lives and facilitating lasting change in others'.

In the last 20 years, I have studied many 'personal growth' techniques, including those where participants leave a course or seminar on a high, believing in, or experiencing, change in certain aspects of their lives. How often have I seen these same people, months later, displaying the same old feelings of unresourcefulness and talking eloquently of all that is wrong with their lives?

I had become something of a sceptic, even on my own optimistic journey, until I met my life-partner, Heather Summers. She too had tried many different techniques. She handed me '*Frogs into Princes*' (Bandler & Grinder, Real People Press, 1979). I read it from cover to cover. I was captivated both by the simplicity and the reality of what was a transcript of one of their seminars. Trying the methods described, I began to see not only new possibilities, but also lasting change in my attitudes and behaviours.

Since then, Heather and I have been through NLP Practitioner and Master Practitioner courses, drawing on both the original 'tools and techniques' approach and the growing therapeutic knowledge and understanding.

Using what we have learned to some degree every day, we have seen, felt and heard of lasting change in our lives and others'. It works, because it goes to the core of how we language and behave.

The Brain, the Mind and the computer analogy

Many people talk of the mind and brain synonymously. A growing number recognise not only the difference, but also the 'mind-body' connection. Much research is still based on the comparison between the brain and the computer. Let's be clear. The brain has a computing function, but no computer has its own feelings or discreet choice (especially irrational), separate from whoever originally programmed it.

NLP has been around for nearly 10 years longer than the PC. The latter has become central to our lives and yet, it merely automates processes that we have the brain capacity to do ourselves. The PC represents the consummation of the 'left-brained' world we have created for ourselves. Yet, while computers can process our trading or investment decisions, they cannot make them without knowing our instructions or priorities. Furthermore, they cannot anticipate our feelings or emotions, whether things are going well or ill.

Feelings are in the mind. They are born of emotional experiences in the past. Where these were 'significant' (in their context at the time), they may have laid down patterns of behaviour, which seem to run themselves. When you feel yourself suddenly moved by an experience, where does that feeling come from? If you have ever felt fear, especially of failure or rejection, where did that originate? We could spend ages philosophising over inherited traits and environment. As a reader of this book, you want to resolve the negative patterns, reinforce or install new positive patterns, so as to maximise your chances of success in trading.

Most of you may have had the experience of losing money through trading at some time. Without that experience, how do we learn? The expert may tell us that we cannot all make money, because the percentages of losses and gains even themselves out over the long term.

Dear reader, you have bought this book to beat those percentages. You may already know or have seen some 'dumb' traders. Even people who have clearly defined strategies may have been distracted by fear, greed or self-delusion to make an irrational trading decision that departed from such strategy.

Why do we make apparent errors of judgement? What is it that drives our decisions, rational or irrational? This book will not only help you to answer those questions, but will also give you the tools to change the patterns as you wish. Even computer driven trades can be beaten. Thousands of people who 'punt' the markets every day are simply 'going to the races'. The stocks they trade are 'horses' in a race where, while there may be many winners, there are more potential losers than in any race card.

The maths and the information are much more complex. The form is harder to study. Many of the tipsters perform worse than the market as a whole. Most important, however, is that where the big punter at the races may bet a day's wages, the day trader may bet the value of their house, or their entire savings. Compulsive gambling has destroyed relationships and families. With day trading, the daily stakes may be very much higher than other forms of gambling. The difference is that the odds are much better at day trading and you do not have to lose everything on one trade.

I promise you this. If you approach day trading as if it were a profession; invest the same effort in understanding how markets work; determine a rational trading strategy and stick to it; understand yourself, through the medium of this book - what your potential 'achilles heels' are and what are your best skills and most resourceful behaviours; you can change not only the success ratio of your trading, but also your whole life and personal relationships. The choice is yours.

So many people study a sound methodology, fail to understand it or apply it objectively, or stick to what is recommended, consequently blaming it when things go wrong. If this has ever fitted you, realise now that it is yourself that you are blaming. We have choices in life about everything we do. As soon as we see that, our lives will have changed forever.

The paradox is realising that being in control is about letting go. Letting go of old beliefs and behaviours that never worked or have outlived their purpose. Letting go of negative scripts and replacing them with or reinforcing the positive patterns.

I exhort you to read this book in one go. It contains many practical exercises you can use to create lasting change in every aspect of your life - especially trading. As with so many study texts, if you try to change everything with only half the story, you may not achieve even half your potential. NLP is wholly about how you think, language and behave. When you (and, if you wish, those nearest to you), will understand yourself better, will have chosen the ways to change your life and effected those changes, and particularly when you have experienced the lasting success and the positive gains, doesn't that sound like a compelling vision for you now?

NLP is a very specific subject. I write and speak using a number of NLP based styles. One of them is called 'Milton Language'. This is a way of communicating to induce a trance like state. It has been shown that trance is the ideal 'learning state'.

As you read this book, you will come across many, very deliberate variations of the traditional grammatical rules on punctuation and mixing up tenses. NLP for Traders has been written to work subliminally, as well as consciously to produce an entirely positive set of beliefs and states in the mind of the reader.

Chapter 1

What do you want to be - a winner?

What's your mission - in trading and in life?

Ask yourself this? For what purpose, for myself, do I exist on this earth? Have you ever asked that? Robert Dilts, one of the great NLP teachers of our time has evolved the concept of logical levels of change. They form a pyramid of contexts for choices and behaviours in our lives:

Mission
Identity - who am I?
Beliefs & Values - why am I doing this?
Capabilities - how and how well do I do things?
Behaviours - what do I do; how do I think/communicate?
Environment - what results do I get when I do all these things?

The higher up the pyramid that we make changes in any aspect of our lives, the greater the overall effect. The first four levels influence all of our behaviours. The results we get are experienced in our immediate environment, in which we interact with other people. It is hard to change other people. We all have our own will and model of the world. If you're not getting the results you expect, or want, try different behaviours. The best and most lasting way is to make change at the highest level.

Some years ago, I had lost my job and had no idea what I was going to do next. One day, I took a sheet of paper and divided it into four. In the first quadrant, I listed all the things I enjoyed doing. In the second, I wrote all the things I was good at. Then, I listed everything that I had the capability of doing which made money. Finally, I wrote down what was important to me in my life, in relation to my mission. I then crossed out everything that didn't appear on all four lists.

As I write, I am practising one of those six activities. I enjoy them all, I have a 'portfolio career' and they all make money. You can do the same.

If you trust in serendipity, that is what you may get. Was it Gary Player or Jack Nicklaus who was accused of being a 'lucky golfer'? "Sure, and I've noticed that the harder I practice, the luckier I get..."

What are you projecting about yourself, in your life, right now? In my experience, people who expect problems somehow seem to get them. If you see yourself as unsuccessful in relationships, for example, what seems to happen? How much of your expectations are you 'wearing' in your body language?

For too long, I was worried about losing money through day trading. I checked the prices many times a day. When I saw a loss, I broke my own 'stop-loss' rules and clung on as the stock fell, watching the deficit grow. Not only did I invariably lose more money than I had planned, but I also had capital tied up when other, better prospects came along. I ended up putting my wife into these good stocks and she made a fortune. When I had even a small gain for myself, however, I would often take it, fearful that it would disappear.

I had been running an unresourceful mental strategy, which conflicted with my rational trading strategy. Having been burnt in the past, my unconscious mind delivered exactly what I feared. Then I discovered NLP and began to rewrite the script. I decided to change the previous pattern of behaviour. Two days later, three of my stocks were in the top ten movers of the day!

Life is a movie. You are the scriptwriter, the director and the principal actor. If some of the negative movies we run in our lives were shown at the cinema every week, a second Great Depression would be upon us in no time.

One of the most powerful processes described in this book is visualisation, or envisioning. When you have mastered your own positive self-beliefs, you may be delighted at how easily you can project positive outcomes and have them fulfilled. If you have children, or a partner, try thinking ill of them for a short period and then think only the best and notice the difference in what happens around you.

So, for what purpose for yourself would you want to run a negative movie about your trading? Do you want to lose money? Do you enjoy it? Do you fascinate other people with your tales of woe, or would you like to be seen as a winner? Don't tell me you behave like that on the golf course as well? I shall use analogies from golf from time to time because like trading, golf is a microcosm of life. (This is the subject of one of my other books, *Change Your Life, Change Your Golf*)

Do you cheer people up when you tell them about your losses? Maybe they feel reassured that there are other 'losers' around. Do you, or they, only talk about 'the one that got away', or have you dined out for too long on the lucky killing you made? When you make a big profit, do you become bolder and raise the stakes, or do you sell enough stock to leave you in for free?

When I first went to college I got in with a crowd who played a card game called brag. Everyone got three cards. The rules were similar to poker. If you looked at your cards, you had to bet twice the stake that you paid to 'go blind'. Based on statistics, 'going blind' was idiotic. Eventually, I worked out that I could make a steady income from joining a game where the majority used this strategy. One night, I was scared rigid when a fellow student lost his entire grant cheque. I never played again.

When you make a trade, do you research the prospect, or play a hunch? Some years ago, I was Treasurer of a major finance house. My job was to trade a $10 billion portfolio daily. Sometimes I played a hunch and won big. Occasionally, I would go inside and check if it was OK and my mind knew that when I had time to retrospectively work out the rationale, it would stack up.

So how did I do it? First, I was instinctively good at maths. Second, I spent most of the day reading the financial press and talking to people whose views I respected. By the time I made the trade, my mind had assimilated all the data and spotted the opportunity on the screen.

The man who came to change the lighting strip one day nearly fell off his ladder when he heard the deals I was doing. "How do you do that and sleep at night?" he said. "Other people's money" said I. It was true. I worried about my own money and made impromptu, uninformed, blind speculations. With the company's money, I was a trained professional, doing the best I could for 10 hours a day.

That's the difference. Successful day trading is a full-time or heavy part-time occupation. It is a job in its own right. If you are betting your house or your savings, why would you approach it with any less diligence than your day job? Professional gamblers regard their pursuit as nothing less than a full-time occupation.

So what is your mission in life? How does your trading fit with, facilitate or reinforce it? What is your philosophy in life and how does this compare to your trading philosophy? Does anything you are doing go counter to that mission or your stated values? If it does, at the very least, you may be accumulating unconscious stress. Are you really a winner, or are you a loser on a winning streak? If the losses start, will you double up until the table in front of you and your pockets are empty?

So what's the secret? The secret is in your self. You have all the skills, ability and potential you need. Whether you recognise that you have the specific capabilities or not, the way that you are made means that you have the observation, assimilation, decision and implementation skills to watch and model what works beyond question for others.

After mission comes identity. After you ask yourself the question "for what purpose do I exist" ask yourself "who am I?" Pretty quickly you can define yourself in terms of a set of Values, Beliefs and Attitudes. When we talk about goals for your life and your trading later, you will automatically set these in the context of your values, attitudes and beliefs.

What's missing? Is it based on a limiting belief - "oh I couldn't do that because...?" You have independence of thought and action. Life is a voyage of self-discovery. When you will have read this book, what positive thoughts and aspirations do you already sense that you want to have achieved? When you have seen your success, what are you saying to yourself now? That's right....

So how are you not already achieving this?

"You have advanced to the hardest part of trading - being able to live with your trading decisions. Experienced traders are finally realising that a proper psychological attitude is essential to successful trading... Trading is much more than simply applying a trading method and watching profits grow in your account. It is a constant struggle where the battleground is not the market but always within you."

In his excellent text, *The Elements of Successful Trading* (NYIF, 1992), quoted above, Robert P Rotella introduces psychology as 'the heart of trading'. He identifies three behavioural traits: emotions; philosophy; and intelligence.

Daniel Goleman wrote about '*Emotional Intelligence*' (Bantam Books, 1995). In NLP, we learn about the importance of self-mastery. Above all: an awareness of your self and the impact you have on others; an ability to listen to language, calibrate

14

neurophysiology and understand the basis of human behaviour; a recognition of choice and the ability to flex your behaviour as appropriate; will help you succeed as a trader, no less than an intimate understanding of markets and what drives them.

Indeed, trading is a microcosm, even a magnified view of life. Situations and emotions can develop just as fast as in life. Stress is a given factor. Money is the driving force and when one's livelihood or even total net worth are on the line, the ability to be 'above all this' is critical. How about you?

There is a view that the October 1987 Crash was due not just to computer driven trades, but also to traders who had never lived through a bear market, were used to seeing prices steadily progressing and sold on fear. In 1929, it was beyond belief that the market could fall for people who had pledged their life savings and even borrowed to invest in a 'one way market'.

"If you can keep your head when all about you are losing theirs..." In *If*, Rudyard Kipling also wrote...

> *If you can make one heap of all your winnings*
> *And risk it on one turn of pitch-and-toss,*
> *And lose, and start again at your beginnings*
> *And never breathe a word about your loss...*
> *Yours is the Earth and everything that's in it,*
> *And - which is more - you'll be a Man, my son!"*

Many successful millionaires lost one or several fortunes before they made it big. Jeffrey Archer lost everything gambling on a speculative oil investment. His response was to write a book *Not a Penny More, Not a Penny Less*, based on his experiences. Warner Brothers gave him a $400,000 advance for the film rights. He went on to become a best-selling author and multi-millionaire! To succeed after total or even substantial loss requires great self-mastery and emotional intelligence. This book will also help you to avoid such a situation in the first place.

How do you handle loss - or fear of loss?

To Mark Barton - and to many others - losing one's life savings must seem like total catastrophe. So much of one's self may be bound up in trading. To win big means a huge boost to the ego. To lose, and keep losing, may go to the very core of our being. We cannot afford for trading to totally reflect ego in this way. What do we have to prove to ourselves, when we are alive and well? Even when we do not feel well, especially when we are stressed, what are we thinking and feeling to create this 'dis-ease'?

The money creation process is infinite. If the market believes that an Internet stock with no earnings in the foreseeable future is worth 100 times what it was worth last year, then that is its worth. We created it between us. The process of inflation, at a micro or macro level, is a process of creating illusory wealth. When you come to cash your chips, however, especially when you are ahead of the game, that wealth buys real material possessions.

So what is losing money, when money and wealth creation are so easy? The process of losing money is not misfortune, it is mistaken, misinformed or misguided decisions. And who makes the decisions. Even if you give your investments to others to manage, you are wholly responsible for that decision.

Your decision to trade your wealth, directly or indirectly, is yours and yours alone. Begin by accepting that you are responsible for all your own choices, consciously or unconsciously, that you are at cause for everything that happens in your life and we shall show you how you can create and protect your wealth. It springs from you and through the tools and techniques of NLP, you can better understand you and win for you and your stakeholders.

When you will have read this book and in some future time you are applying its sound wisdom, you can go forward to some future time and see yourself trading soundly and profitably. Now that you have seen that vision and enjoyed the success it has brought, how do you feel about your ability to be a winner now? That's right....

the unconscious mind notices the patterns, makes the connections and guides your judgement.

We are all one with the universe. Preoccupation with self takes from the rest. "True self-interest teaches selflessness. Heaven and earth endure because they are not simply selfish but exist in behalf of all creation. The wise leader, knowing this, keeps egocentricity in check and by doing so becomes even more effective." (John Heider, *The Tao of Leadership,* Gower 1993).

You can be a leader in every aspect of your life. The calm, quiet leader is best, always believing that there is more to learn, more to know. For the now, all that matters is the now. Visualise and programme your future and your unconscious mind will sort that out. The past can't be changed and the future is unknowable. You can only do and be the best you can be.

"Prosperity is not defined by money alone; it encompasses time, love, success, joy, comfort, beauty and wisdom... Know what your beliefs are, they can be changed in this moment. The power that created you has given you the power to create your own experiences. You can change!" (*Louise Hay, Love Yourself, Heal Your Life,* Hay House Inc, 1990).

Louise Hay also says that the power of the future is in this moment. Fear, of failure, rejection, or whatever, is a future emotion. It may be based on emotional experiences from the past and you may feel the emotion in the present. It is an emotion about something that has not happened yet, and may not. So why worry? Live your life in the present moment and start to visualise your inevitable success and, having done so, enjoy the pleasure of anticipation as you diligently build that success right now.

NLP - a model of Excellence

NLP began with Bandler and Grinder studying what made people excellent. Once upon a time, it was believed that only a handful of people on the planet could ski excellently well. Then, we started to film and video these gods of skiing. By freeze framing and breaking down the constituent parts of the skiing process into their basic elements, schools of skiing evolved. Now, my 70 year old mother can go on a holiday and learn to ski.

Similarly, Bandler and Grinder studied Erickson, Satir, Perls and Bateson to understand what made them excellent in their own fields. Primarily, this was based on listening to language patterns and calibrating the neurophysiology which characterised their behaviour pattern. When they had disaggregated the elements of external and internal language and behaviours upon which the excellence was based, they then set about modelling these to achieve similar results.

Personal development through NLP is based on: understanding our own patterns of language and behaviour; their internal meanings; ways in which they can be made more resourceful and effective; and a set of tools and techniques to implement changes we choose to make for ourselves. This book will help you to understand and apply most of the main techniques of NLP to your trading and thereby your life.

In trading, investment and in life, there are many role models of excellence. By observing and understanding their patterns of behaviour; by listening to their language patterns and calibrating their neurophysiology, you could gain an understanding sufficient to use as a basis for installing excellent behaviours in your self.

Normally, the full NLP based approach is to work with a compliant subject using a patient and detailed questioning process to elicit, understand and where appropriate enhance the strategies and patterns of behaviour that are the basis of excellence. Then, by consciously learning and repeating these elements until they become unconsciously installed, the excellent behaviour can be modelled.

The pattern we shall follow in the remainder of this book is based on the client centred NLP approach I would use, whether coaching team or individual in an organisation or working with someone in therapy.

We begin by understanding the power of the unconscious mind. The filters through which all sensory input are processed include primarily our values and beliefs. These are the basis of our patterns of behaviour, whether resourceful or not. Having helped the client to understand these patterns, we then move towards their goals and achievable outcomes they would like to set themselves. The present context would of course be trading.

The values and beliefs work often uncovers limiting decisions and beliefs from childhood. When we have worked to help the client make new choices to remove or modify these they can begin to see a way of achieving success. Understanding and applying the tools and techniques of NLP can lead to a state of self mastery. When this has been achieved, we examine the strategies applied in a particular aspect of the person's life where they would like to achieve change. Unpacking these strategies, reviewing them and modifying them as appropriate can lead to more resourceful behaviour.

Sometimes the behaviour may still be inappropriate to the desired result. The range of NLP techniques has grown exponentially in its 27 years of life. One of its presuppositions is that continuing flexibility of language and behaviour will produce better and more lasting positive results than merely replicating the previous unresourceful patterns of behaviour.

While it is possible to install or enhance self-confidence, sometimes, especially in potentially stressful situations such as trading, old negative beliefs and patterns may have got in the way. As the pursuit of reward accelerated the attendant risks may have crept into awareness. Fear of loss or failure, where they existed, could have been demotivating, stressful and have inhibited the achievement of success. Self-confidence and self-esteem may not always have been sufficient to override irrational patterns of emotions from the past. There are a number of interventions which can change these permanently.

In order to create a lasting change, you may wish to use a variety of approaches which best suit you. Modelling can be highly successful. In addition, using positive anchors to utilise powerful resourceful states of achievement from the past, together with reframing apparent negative situations to see the positive aspects and opportunities for learning can lead to a continuous cycle of success.

Finally, you may already have perceived the possibilities of integrating NLP into a whole new regime of life, both for your trading and in general. The regular use of meditation and exercise, together with a balanced diet, can also help the trader or anyone for that matter to be more energetic, calmer, more resilient and better able to manage stress and whatever challenges may arise from day-to-day.

Chapter 2

Who are you - what's your psychological make-up?

The psychology of trading is the psychology of beliefs, strategies and behaviours

Why do you want to trade? What happened if you lost-how did it affect you? It depends on your psychological make-up. If you had a fear of losing, or failure, this may have built upon itself. If you are more resourceful in such circumstances, loss can be an opportunity for learning.

"Trading is a mental and physical game which provides an intellectual, physical and emotional challenge of the highest order." (Robert P Rotella, *ibid.*).

Our psychology determines the way we trade, the way we approach risk, how we respond to volatility and how we deal with losses if they occur. The gambler may approach trading with an attitude of trying to maximise profits. If you are risk averse you may try to minimise losses. The approach I have used both as a corporate and individual trader is to optimise the gains at a managed level of risk. Analysis can help to understand and minimise the risk, otherwise you may be taking unknown or unreasonable risks in the pursuit of gain.

Your trading outlook will inevitably reflect, to some degree, your outlook on life in general and the beliefs set that you hold. The question is how well can you balance logic and intuition.

Limiting beliefs and negative emotions may go hand in hand. If your script has been dominated by fear of failure, you may (as I once did) have run your losses and grabbed your gains, however small.

Your prospects for success will improve immeasurably when you realise that ultimately you determine the success or failure of your trading (assuming that you have enough capital in the first place). Trading will test your resilience and find out your emotions and feelings. Ideally, therefore you should approach the process with positive feelings and in a resourceful state. If not, you may want to question whether now is the time to trade.

It has often been said that a car in the hands of an upset person could have been as lethal as a gun. For some people, trading has been a life or death experience, especially where the limits were stretched.

Your attitudes and beliefs in general will have a significant impact in determining your ability to stick to your chosen trading strategy and methodology. When you can calmly and objectively decide on the signals and take timely action as appropriate, you are reducing the element of luck and increasing your prospects of success.

Psychological make-up includes not only emotion, but also philosophy of life and what Goleman called emotional intelligence - the gravitas of the leader; the rational calmness of the professional trader.

Stock and money markets can sometimes resemble battlefields. Volatility is much greater than it used to be. Violent swings from gain to loss and back again can now occur in a single trading day. Getting the movement right is the way successful day traders make their money. Coolness under fire is a fundamental requirement. "If you can't stand the heat, stay out of the kitchen."

In *The Four Fold Way* (Harper Collins, 1993), Angeles Arrien describes four personality types: the warrior, the healer, the visionary, and the teacher. These derive from the shaman traditions of all races and have been handed down to us through time immemorial. The warrior lives in the present moment; the healer pays attention to what has meaning; the visionary sees and tells truth without judgement; the teacher is open to outcome, not attached to it. These are the basis of holistic wisdom.

In the ancient world and even until the last century, it was a man's role to be a hunter. This ingrained characteristic has sometimes been a nuisance in both personal life and trading. It may have made us unnecessarily aggressive. It was the basis of macho behaviours, sometimes leading to the mindless pursuit of a result when wisdom should have prevailed.

Filters - values and beliefs

In this book we shall introduce many of the presuppositions of NLP. These will be identified by a sub script Px. The first of these is:

P1　The map is not the territory

We try to understand people based on what we see and hear. In NLP this is called the shallow structure. It does give some insights into the real person before us, but some language and behaviour is unconsciously created to disguise or conceal aspects of the real personality. Extraversion, for example, may conceal a shy person.

The deep structure is largely composed of our values, attitudes and beliefs. Sometimes we ourselves may not be consciously aware either of these or the behaviours that others perceive. What we do know is that our deep structure will unconsciously influence our behaviour in trading.

These values and beliefs were laid down in the first 21 years of our lives - sometimes called the socialisation period. Our parents or surrogates were the prime influence in our first seven years. In the next seven years, our school, siblings and peers. Finally, society and its institutions. We can change these values and beliefs.

People are not their behaviours. The language and behaviours only give clues to the whole person. Depending on their programming from their formative years, people will behave differently in different circumstances and with different people. You may come to understand this more clearly as this book unfolds. You may already be getting insights into yourself. You may by now be accepting yourself more. Accept the person and manage their behaviours. That includes you.

P2   Experience has a structure

Our values and beliefs can be changed. All sensory input is reviewed by the mind against existing memories, which are kept in structured patterns. When you change the structure of the memory, you can change how the past is recalled, how the present is experienced and how the future is expected. I will leave it to you to anticipate the positive opportunities for your trading and your life.

Our beliefs and values are recognised in our internal dialogue, as well as our external language and behaviour. Is our self-talk positive, or negative? If it is negative, and especially critical, STOP IT NOW. How often do you use imperatives in your self-talk - "I must do this, I should do that, I've got to do this, I shouldn't have done that..."- as opposed to choices: "I can do this, I may do that, I would like to do this, I choose to do that..." If someone, who you know loves you or cares about you, were to talk to you in the way you may have sometimes criticised or otherwise beaten yourself up, how would you feel?

Start now to change your internal dialogue to loving and caring. See and feel the immediate and lasting changes in your outlook on life, your behaviours and attitudes to other people.

Another tenet of NLP is:

P3   Perception is projection

There is a traditional equivalent - 'it takes one to know one'. If you are tempted to criticise or speak negatively about someone else, try it on in the first person and see if that changes your perception of you - and them. As someone once said "be kind to yourself, because wherever you go, there you are."

Whether on the golf course, the trading floor, the tennis court, or in life in general, be kind to yourself, because every time you criticise or berate yourself, you may be reinforcing exactly the behaviours you might wish to be rid of. People who expect problems somehow seem to get them, sometimes repeatedly!

P4   The effect is not the problem - the cause is

Pleasant or unpleasant situations may trigger states in a person. Sometimes unresourceful behaviours may result.   In such circumstances the person may be 'at effect'. The surface effect is merely an indication of the deeper cause. If we have found ourselves at effect in a trading situation in the past, an insight into the originating cause may help us to choose more productive behaviour in future. When you are able to live any aspect of your life at cause, then you may be able to achieve the short or long term goals you desire.

P5   All meaning is context dependent

As Tad James, the famous NLP exponent is fond of saying "there is no content in content worth knowing". Any word is meaningless without a context or reference. If I use the word blue, you might think I am talking about the colour of the sky. I may in fact be thinking about sadness.   In a dictionary, words are defined in relation to context.

A thought you think, or something you hear, will be interpreted depending on the assumed or actual context. In an open outcry market, shouting or hollering may be the accepted norm. In a relationship, it would probably be wholly undesirable.

Think now of a pleasurable experience from your past, where you felt great energy and resourcefulness. In this positive context, such behaviour may be entirely appropriate. Reflect for a moment on the positive changes you can make in your trading all your life when you can transfer such a positive state into what previously might have been a negative situation.

P6 Presuppositions of choice

We always make the best choices available to us in a given state or circumstances. As you improve your self mastery, you will become aware of opportunities to make different, more productive choices. Any choice is better than no choice and all procedures should increase choice.

Whether trading or in life in general, living one's life at cause means by definition making more choices. If you knew someone who appeared to be at effect, their life may appear to run itself. If you always are what you always were you may always get what you always got.

If your trading has been less successful than you wished, recognise your responsibility for your own life and decisions, move to cause, make more informed and productive choices and see the consequent benefits flow for you.

P7 Underlying every behaviour is a positive intent

Our patterns of behaviour are the result of patterns and programs acquired during our childhood and youth. When we have been momentarily at effect, a state may have emerged from our subconscious, based on these patterns. This did not mean that we wanted the consequent negative result. Have you ever asked yourself "where did that come from?" Have you ever felt yourself to be misunderstood.

Think of an aspect of your past behaviour that you would like to have changed. Ask yourself repeatedly, "for what highest positive purpose for myself did I do that?"

This process is known as 'chunking up'. As you ask the question, your internal answers should become more abstract. Here is a hypothetical internal dialogue for someone who has made an error of judgement trading: "For what purpose for myself did I make that error of judgement?

- I was frightened that I would lose my gain.
- Why was I frightened?
- Because I don't like to lose.
- For what purpose for myself do I not like to lose?
- I want to be a winner.
- Why do I want to be a winner?
- Because I want people to respect me.
- Why do I want people to respect me?
- Because I want to be accepted
- Why do I want to be accepted?
- Because I want to be happy."

So the process ends in a highest positive intent. When you reach happiness, love, or something of equivalent abstraction, you may well be at the highest positive intent. Try it now and realise the positive purposes that have driven any previous unresourceful behaviours.

P8   The meaning of your communication is the response you get

You cannot not communicate. What do I mean? If you and I were sat together now, having a discussion, only 7% of your understanding would come from the actual words I said. (There is no content ...). Another 38% would come from the tonality I used in saying the words and 55% would come from my 'neurophysiology'.

When you watched Bill Clinton on the Lewinsky tapes, why did there seem to be more meaning than the words themselves conveyed. Did you watch his eye movements, hear him clear his throat, adjust his posture, etc. Part of the reason of course, is that you are interpreting all the input you receive through your own model of the world. We shall see how to change that in perceptual positions.

If we ever misunderstood someone's meaning, maybe it was because we 'mind-read' them. Maybe we unconsciously or intuitively read the 'body language' (neurophysiology) and put our own interpretation on it.

Have you ever asked your partner or friend, " what's wrong?" simply because you felt you had an idea that something was not quite right. It may have been as much in what Mr Clinton didn't say as what he said, that we formed our own ideas of the truth. If he had sat there saying nothing to each question, his 'body language' would be communicating some form of message. If only we could understand. People cannot not communicate. Later, I shall tell you how to interpret these signals.

Resistance is a sign of a lack of rapport. If you do not get the response you intend, it is more than just the words that are involved. "Don't shout so loud, I can't hear you!" If someone grew up around anger, they may have learned at an early age to 'switch off' to loud behaviour.

Later, we shall learn about eye accessing cues and predicates, so that you can choose to modify your behaviour and communication to achieve the desired response.

P9   There is no failure, only feedback

Failure is an attitude of mind. One person may see another as a failure, in their model of the world. The subject may not see things that way. They may not feel a failure; they may have a very positive disposition, seeing every shortfall on desired or planned performance as an opportunity to learn. So it may be with your trading.

If someone saw and continued to see their shortfalls as failure, they may simply be reinforcing a 'program' laid down in childhood. Every situation in life presents opportunities to learn and, if we choose, to modify behaviour. Seeing a shortfall as failure is likely to result from feelings of being at effect (P4). Putting Oneself at cause - anything that varies from the planned, or expected outcomes - is an opportunity to review, reappraise, modify, beliefs and behaviours.

Try this model when you are offering feedback yourself (especially to children):

- This is what specifically went well.
- These are possibilities for you to improve. Overall, this is how well you performed.

Watch the change in response as the person begins to recognise the chance of learning and growing.

If you ever lost money on a trade, what was there for you to learn? Where could you have improved? Frankly and candidly, how well did you do overall. Are you going to grab the opportunities to learn and grow, resulting in increasing success in the longer term. After all, the chart of the market may seesaw, but given enough time, it continues inexorably upwards. It must, until inflation is permanently eliminated. How well is your own long-term chart performing?

If you were to go forward to a time when you could look back and see that, around this time, the chart of your personal fortunes and well-being had broken out into a new and powerful uptrend, as a result of understanding the messages in this book, how does that feel for you right now?

P10 If what you are doing isn't working, do something else...anything else!

If your trading strategy, style or methodology isn't producing the results you desire, or expect, you could review every aspect of what you are doing.

This includes not only the mechanical, numerical, analytical and other things you are doing in the trading specifics, it also includes what you are doing in and with yourself. You will understand more as the book unfolds.

P11 The Law of Requisite Variety

This Law comes from cybernetics. Basically it means that the person and/or system with the greatest flexibility and/or adaptability will end up controlling the system. Try varying every aspect of what you do, dry-running it against actual market conditions before you implement it in practice.

Also, as the above implies, if it's not working, try anything else until it does. However, 'if it ain't broke don't fix it'.

P12 People work perfectly - we already have all the resources we need

The question is do we realise this; have we accepted it? Are you at cause or effect in your life? Be at cause and take responsibility for everything that you do. Choose your behaviours and watch a new more purposeful life unfold for you.

P13 If one person can do something, anyone can learn to do it

You will understand and realise the possibilities more and more as you are reading this book. By the time you have come to modelling, having understood everything that went before, you will be realising the possibilities right now.

P14   All procedures should increase wholeness

Evaluate your behaviour and make the changes appropriate to the context in which you find yourself. Have respect for other people's model of the world. You may not like it, or agree with it, but if you understand it, you have a choice as to whether to respond to it, go with it, go against it, ignore it, etc.

P15   The Mind and Body are part of the same system

You are responsible for your conscious and your unconscious mind and therefore the results that you get. We already know that mind power can control or eliminate illness and disease after it has set in. How many more possibilities can you see when you eliminate it before it occurs.

Norman Vincent Peale wrote of the power of positive thinking. There is now a vast amount of documentary evidence of the powerful positive effects of the unconscious mind. It is also beyond question that the mind and body are part of the same system, now that you are making it work for you...

Values, Beliefs and Meta Programs

Some people believe success and failure are a matter of luck. Others believe in the value of a proven methodology, religiously adhered to. Many people have lost money despite diligent research, a sound method and strict adherence.

When the market suddenly breaks out downwards and a trader finds himself or herself overexposed, even the best trading method may not prevent substantial losses. For example, can you find a buyer for your stock at the price you want? Are you prepared to cut and run, or are you inclined to hold on?

Success and failure are defined by you, and you alone. You set the parameters. If you have been concerned about how others see you, or to be measured by others' measures of performance, how much more can you do when you set the rules of the game? However you see others, or imagine that they see you, you can only process these perceptions through your own model of the world.

If you believe that you can be successful, or, better still, if you believe you are successful, that is all that matters (assuming you are applying rational thought).

Values

Each of us is made up of a set of values and beliefs. In the 30 day programme, you will find how to elicit your own. What are your values set for life; for relationships; for trading? Are your values 'towards' or 'away from' values. When you talk of success, as a value for trading, are you, deep inside, moving towards success, or away from failure? When you have understood your values set; when you have changed or modified these, substantially towards and based on positive language, then you have increased your prospect of success.

We can all choose, whether or not we wish to change. Because you want to succeed, do everything you can to change your internal dialogue and your beliefs to positive... permanently.

We discussed earlier, logical levels of change. As we move more towards mission and identity; as we move more towards spirit and abstraction, so we move more towards our higher self. It is in the higher self that we find our essential morality and goodness and the highest motives for achievement, fulfilment and happiness. Are your values aligned with each other?

As you look at your values set, which is the most abstract. Ideally your most important value should be. As you look down the list, does each successive value support the fulfilment of the next higher, or highest? Consider the underlying motivation for each value. Does it support what you really want? Are there any apparent or actual conflicts between your values? Is there any one value that on its own could prevent you having another at the same time?

towards or away from, etc. in a given set of circumstances. Recognise your own meta-programs, using the section at the back. Change them or make them work for you, as you think appropriate.

As you may have recognised from two of the examples given above, the MBTITM (Myers-Briggs Type Indicators) profiles are part of our meta-programs. The other MBTI pairs are intuitor/ sensor and judger/perceiver. These and some other psychometric assessment methodologies are based on the work of Carl Jung.

Meta program analysis can be carried out faster and can go much beyond MBTI and other psychometric profiling. Some NLP analysts have identified up to 60 different meta programs. We use much less than this number at the back of the book, but sufficient for you to identify the major filter set, which with your values and beliefs can be used to understand, explain and also as the basis of modification for, your personality and thereby trading and personal success. The most important thing is that any change you make should be an informed choice, recognising the positive gains and new possibilities, which can flow from these.

As I will assert over and over, you are at cause not effect. You can be at cause in everything that you do. As you realise this, becoming calmer and with greater self-mastery, you can dramatically influence your performance in trading and life. As you go forward to a time when you have made your own choices and owned the consequences of your soundly based decisions, how many new possibilities for gain in all aspects of your life are you seeing.

Meanwhile, the herd instinct may prevail elsewhere. I know how hard it may have been in the past to run against the crowd, or detach myself from the prevailing market 'wisdom' or belief and stick to my own strategy and methodology. When you rely on others, you will experience the consequences of their decisions (being at effect). Blaming them would be pointless and fruitless.

I remember buying shares in a company tipped in the English Times as 'the best bid story in the market'. They went down and down. I doggedly held on for nearly a year and eventually got out even. The company is still independent. The Times may have carried the article, but it was my choice to invest...and to hang on...and to sell. Others who held off and bought after the shares fell could have made 100 to 200% gain. I made nothing.

You are responsible for the timing, direction, rationale and consequences of a trade. By all means read and listen to the rational or irrational opinions of analysts, experts. You may succeed handsomely, and I can tell you as a former stockbroker that advising clients when to sell is the hardest decision there is. Get it wrong by one pip and someone will be unhappy.

I am an advocate of reading and understanding as much market wisdom as you have the time to. Absorb it, put it to one side and make your own, calm, rational decisions, in keeping with your strategy and methodology. Why do you think the phrases E&OE and caveat emptor appear in commercial law?

In summary, identify your values and beliefs and recognise your meta programs. Change them if you want and/or make them work for you. By understanding them alongside your rational market behaviours you can succeed and have fun doing it. What's more, don't be surprised if other people notice the positive changes that are taking place in your whole personality and relationships with other people.

Mind and Body, Intelligence and Emotions

So, do you possess the traits for trading? Can you acquire them? Do you want to? They are a fundamental component of your character and personality. We have seen the possibility of modifying values and beliefs to create the positive patterns that underlie success in trading and in life.

One of the presuppositions of NLP is that the mind and body are part of the same system. There is daily growing evidence of the effect of positive beliefs on health and well-being. Unfortunately, there is also worrying information about the effect of negative beliefs. On the plus side, the universal average for the 'placebo effect' is about 37%.

We may have conventionally believed that the mind was in and associated with the brain. Certainly there are elements of and processing centres for aspects of mind, in the brain. The mind is distributed throughout our physical whole, however. For example, every nerve cell has its own intelligence and, sufficiently nourished, could survive independently. If your body was dipped in a magic fluid, which could dissolve everything except your nerve cells, you would still be totally recognisable from the nerve cells alone. There are more nerve cells in the human body than there are stars in the visible sky.

This gives an insight into the phenomenal power of the mind. It has two major components - the conscious and unconscious mind. In addition, there is the higher self. In your lifetime, you may not use more than 5% of your brain. Einstein was found to have a much bigger brain than normal when he died. For a long time, it was thought that this was the reason for his 'super-intelligence'. Then it was realised that as he used it more, it grew more cells.

In experiments, rats' brains have been halved, quartered, even shredded and they have still been able to run a maze they had learned. One man, with an above average IQ and a normal family life, died and was found to have no brain, only the brain stem.

The more we use our mind, the greater the number of connections made. When these unconscious connections are brought into consciousness, then we truly have limitless potential. You may use less than a third of your mind, which is distributed throughout you. As the mind needs new nerve cells and connections, it creates them. In one year's time, every nerve cell in you will have been renewed.

We truly have limitless potential. Our unconscious minds record and remember everything. Each thought, feeling or experience goes into the 'void' to be compared and processed against other thoughts feelings and experiences. They are filtered by our meta-programs, values and beliefs, before influencing our memories, behaviours and states, as appropriate.

When we have found out who we are; accepted ourselves; changed as appropriate to completing the task in hand, or fulfilling our potential, then there is truly no limit to what we can achieve.

The mind is the domain of the emotions. It is the repository of emotional experiences and memories from the past, which have influenced our makeup during our formative years and our states, experiences and behaviours thereafter.

Our philosophies are based on our values and beliefs, whether experienced or handed down. While we may be born with innate intelligence, our experiences and environment can enhance this. Similarly, experiences remain in memory and can influence our minds, manifesting themselves in states, language and behaviours. Stress, where it occurs, may be the result of a triggered emotional experience from the past, a conflict between something which is happening in the now, and is not in keeping with our values and beliefs, etc.

Psychological make-up can be a major factor in trading success. You may have an excellent trading strategy and methodology already. If there were negative elements of your psychological makeup which interfered with your rational decisions and particularly your self-confidence and peace of mind, you may not have been able to fulfil your potential yet. Your intellect and intelligence are important, as is your philosophy of life, but for some, it is emotions and negative emotional experiences that have got in the way, unconsciously replaying unresourceful states or behaviours from the past.

Even intelligence is being re-appraised. As Goleman's work (*ibid.*) has recognised, 'emotional intelligence' may be at least as important as general intelligence in determining successful and appropriate behaviour. General intelligence reposes largely in the brain. Emotional intelligence is seated in the mind.

Much has been written about the different characteristics of the left and right hemispheres of the brain. The left is related to logic, language, rational thought and analysis, together with short-term memory. The right is related to creativity, people-centredness, long-term memory, etc. The ideal is to have both working in harmony. Have you ever played Trivial PursuitTM, been asked a question, had the answer pop into your head and dismissed it in favour of a logical answer, or even a wild guess? Then you found that your first thought had been the right answer.

The right brain is intuitive and inspired, the left brain's logic may have sometimes overridden the best solution or the right path. We can be at our best when left and right brains, conscious and unconscious mind are in harmony. In the program there are some exercises to improve the left/right brain partnership.

Women tend to engage both sides of the brain most of the time. This is because the 'corpus callosum', which connects the two, is far thicker in women than in men. Men are perfectly capable of using either or both hemispheres, but condition and biological makeup has tended in the past to lead to engaging one or other (often the left).

We have nerve cells throughout our brain and, of course our whole body. Each has its own intelligence. The mind cells carry emotional intelligence, experiences and memories. I have heard it said "give me a manager with back pain and I'll show you a manager under stress". It is true that back pain can result from physical injury. The unconscious mind is very clever and in the past, even though the original injury may have healed, the mind may have hooked emotionally painful memories to the muscular seat of the original pain. Then, when internal conflict produced stress, the back pain may have returned, in the guise of muscular tension.

I had back trouble for 10 years. Since experiencing NLP Practitioner and Master Practitioner techniques and NLP based therapies, I have had no recurrence and expect to have a healthy back for the rest of my life. At my most stressful times in the past, I have occasionally been bent double with pain, or muscular seizure. Now I play golf with mental and physical freedom.

If you have an apparent physical infirmity, which may have appeared to manifest itself at times of stress, ask yourself "when did I decide to have this physical difficulty? What was happening in my life in general at that time?" When you have identified the source, you may decide to make some positive changes in your values or beliefs, releasing negative memories or experiences, having preserved the positive learnings. As you think of a time in the future, when you are benefiting from these positive changes, notice how, having experienced the new choices things somehow seem different now....

Freud talked of the ego, id and superego. In NLP, we talk of the conscious mind, the unconscious mind and the higher self. These are the three levels of consciousness. In meditation, you may go from the alpha (or waking) state, to the beta or deeper states. When the unconscious mind is in harmony with the conscious, we have progressed to a deeper state of consciousness, where more learning or understandings may be found.

Hypnosis is trance under another name. Trance is the ideal learning state. Some sports people talk of being in 'the zone' or in 'flow'. These are trance states, where the conscious and unconscious minds can be in harmony. Zen Buddhism, relaxation methods and other trance inducing behaviours may help us to engage the more resourceful sources of our mind, leading to calmer, more centred, more positive behaviours. People may talk of 'being in control'. The paradox is that to be in control we should learn how to let go. Trance is one way to let go.

Some people talk of opportunities and threats, others of opportunities and challenges. Every experience in life produces learning. When you see these in a positive light, you can change and grow. Think of the possibilities and the positives, not the impossibles. Newtonian logic may suggest that there is only black or white for each situation we find ourselves in. Wouldn't life be boring if there weren't shades in between?

If you are sat in a chair, what is 'not chair' - everything else? If the book you are holding looking at and reading to yourself represents success, then what is not success? Everything else. Failure is only one of an infinite number of possibilities, which exist outside of total success. Who defines success and failure for you? - You do. Using Cartesian logic (after Rene Descartes), ask yourself the following questions.

"When I have determined a trading style, strategy and methodology, together with making the positive changes in my values and beliefs to produce the possibility of great success, what will I get as a result?

• What will I not get, as a result of these positive changes?

• What would I have got if I had left things as they were?

• What would I not have got if I had left things as they were?"

And notice the changes and new possibilities that are already opening up before you.

Sometimes, we may choose to go inside, to come outside. For some people, there has been noise inside, which got in the way of clear understanding and positive expectation.

For me, one of the greatest gains from using all the tools and techniques in this book has been the end of the ceaseless internal dialogue and rehearsal, including running negative programs and possibilities, fears and anxieties.

Do you, like many people, have an internal dialogue? Did that inner voice ever speak to you harshly when things appeared to go wrong? Think of someone from your present or past, who you know loves you or cares about you deeply. Imagine if they spoke to you in the way that internal voice may have spoken to you in the past. How would you feel? So, why on earth would you ever have wanted to speak to yourself in the same way? What highest positive purpose could that have served? So...frame it in the positive...

- "What in particular worked well in the exercise or activity I have been engaged in?
- What positive opportunities are there for me to learn, improve and grow?
- Overall, how well did I do?"

When my son was very small, my wife and I separated. He was the innocent victim of the unhappiness at the time. After things had settled down and I saw him every weekend, I invented a game that we played every night that I saw him, for eight years. You could play it with yourself each night, before you sleep:

- "Tell me something good that happened to you today?
- Tell me something good about yourself?
- Tell me something you are looking forward to doing tomorrow?"

Louise Hay has a further suggestion. Each day, find time, on your own, to look in a mirror and say "I love myself and everything about me."

We have discussed perceptual positions elsewhere. Take yourself outside yourself and see who you really are and redefine the possible. The unconscious mind is a reservoir for resourcefulness: mental, emotional, mind/body, spiritual, meditation, self-mastery, awareness, etc. Even physical (diet, sleep, exercise) resourcefulness results directly from positive thoughts, beliefs and expectations.

Create an internal representation of yourself with the physique and weight you want to be. Step into that internal experience, see and feel it through your own eyes. Now let your conscious or unconscious mind choose a time in your future when you want to be this person. Step outside of the internal representation so that you can see yourself, with the physique and weight you will be, and put that vision out into that future time. Relax and let your unconscious mind create that future certainty. It is so powerful that it is impossible to tell the difference between a vivid internal imagined experience and an external real one.

So, create the representation and feeling of what it will be like to be a successful trader and do the same for this, putting this future certainty out into your timeline. Do the other things in this book in your now and start noticing the immediate changes now.

The power of the unconscious mind can be observed in everyday life. One example is 'organ language'. Have you noticed how often people use descriptive language for states or behaviours and somehow that may be related to a physical aspect of their life? For example, "I must try and get my head round this… I don't mind… That was a mindless thing to do… She gets my back up… He's a pain in the butt, etc." Did you ever notice someone who had had physical symptoms in that part of the body or organ which they referred to in their language construction?"

The Brain

We may not even use much of our brain capacity in our lives. Thinking patterns may be related to the brain or the mind. If I asked you what two and two made, you would probably answer four. Sometimes, language or experience can trigger an emotional memory or state, often unconsciously, on its way through processing. This is because everything passes through our filters. Someone who had experienced the break-up of a lifetime relationship in unhappy circumstances, when asked what one and one made, might not automatically have answered two. Indeed, in relationships, sometimes it has made two (partnership), sometimes more than two (synergy), sometimes less (conflict).

For trading, thinking patterns should ideally be 'flat'. If they were tainted by negative emotions, errors of omission or commission might have been the result. Through this book, you will be able to make rational trading decisions, unaffected by negative emotional experiences, memories or states.

This leads me to EQ, or emotional intelligence. Many companies had wondered how extraordinarily intelligent individuals were sometimes capable of stupid or unresourceful decisions or behaviours. Goleman proposed that the emotional component of one's thinking, processing and behaviour was at least as important. For example, if you knew someone who was in the middle of a violent argument, would they ordinarily have been able to sustain rational thinking and behaviour (unless they were a psychopath, for example)?

In the Master Practitioner track of NLP, we talk about achieving self-mastery. This is to be wholly at cause in all things we do. In emotional intelligence terms, I would talk of being able to choose to adopt the most appropriate language and behaviour as appropriate to each situation. The equation can become:

$$Intelligence = IQ + EQ$$

(and now some writers are talking of SQ, or spiritual intelligence)

People also tend to associate the brain with memory. How many times have you heard someone say "I have a poor memory", or "my memory is fading as I get older". These are, of course, limiting beliefs. Nobody need have a poor or declining memory. The unconscious records and remembers everything. In a recent experiment, a probe was inserted into a woman's brain and she recalled in perfect detail, the occasion of her birthday when she was very young, even down to the feel of her party frock.

The skill we are needing is recall. This is simply a learned and mastered set of skills. First, there is the way we record the memory in the first place. The best technique is association. The more connections the brain can hook up to some information, the better it records it, especially by the use of pictures. Improving recall is a matter of understanding and learning the most productive strategy. Elsewhere we have considered eye patterns. If you want to recall a memory with a visual component, look up and to your left. That will connect your thoughts to the visual centres of the brain.

In conclusion, through understanding something of how your mind, body and brain can work in harmony, you may understand that all problems you perceive for yourself in trading markets are actually in yourself. Otherwise they would not be a problem for you. When you looked for problems, you may have found you got them. If you ever programmed yourself for less than the best, you may have got exactly that. If a particular experience upset you, or caused you stress, what were the emotional triggers from the past which, when they were removed, left you only with the positive lessons to be learned?

The market may create a situation that triggers a state, but you decided the strategy, you made and implemented the decision, your acts and will created both the 'problem' and the problem state. Put yourself at cause. Achieve personal mastery and win. Understand the 'problem' and its source and manifestation, or alternatively, reframe it to a more constructive possibility. Put yourself at cause in all you do and see your life as a series of choices.

See your life as a series of choices and change any residual negative patterns which may have existed in the past. Ask yourself the question, how important is it to you to succeed at trading? For what highest purpose for yourself is this important? Note and remove or modify any negative or unresourceful patterns which may have been present.

Use the full power of your general intelligence. Modify your emotional intelligence so that it produces only positive enhancements and behaviours, practice and improve all the powers of your brain. Utilise the limitless positive potential of your mind and succeed on your own terms.

Chapter 3

What do you want to do? - programme a compelling vision

Goals and Outcomes

You are not alone in wanting to trade and make money, so what will set you apart? Going back to levels of change, how do you see yourself as a trader? What is its importance in your life, its purpose and mission? Are your values and beliefs all positive and supportive of the success you want to achieve? Do you have a plan? What long term and intermediate goals have you set yourself? In this chapter we shall also talk about setting and visualising outcomes.

What capabilities do you have for trading successfully and how can you enhance these, both in brain and mind? What purposeful behaviours are you displaying? What language patterns are you using, including internal? Are they positive? How do you perceive the environment in which you are trading? What changes can you make in that environment and especially the way you perceive it, that will help to optimise your performance?

As I am writing this book, I have broken it down into 'bite-size chunks'. That way, I can write up to 8,000 words in a day. I set myself mini-targets during the day, like stepping-stones across the river. As I achieve each of these, I reward myself in some small way - chocolate biscuits with my tea, etc. Also, as I write each idea, all the time I am working towards an ultimate goal, which I have visualised.

As I write, I am also visualising many of the situations I am writing about. My environment is warm, conducive and relaxed. Baroque music is playing (it creates the right brain waves for productivity) and I am relaxed, purposeful and happy.

Any major project or process is enhanced by having a goal or goals to work towards. These may be long, medium or short term - whatever works for you. A friend of mine sits down with his wife every New Year's Day and they work out joint goals together. As they review them, they may wonder if they will achieve them all in one year. Each year, they marvel as they achieve and surpass them.

There is a well-known story about the group of Harvard students, to whom it was suggested they might wish to do a life plan. Many year's later, they were followed up. Only 5-10% had set a plan. Their total income exceeded the total income of the 90% who had not set a plan. Give the unconscious mind a clear set of goals to work towards, turn them into a vivid internal representation, see yourself in the picture, put it out in your future timeline and watch your unconscious mind deliver!

Goal setting is a traditional process for many companies. I used to think the majority would do strategic planning before I became a management consultant. In practice I found only 5% or so carried out a meaningful exercise which they reviewed and renewed annually, monitoring progress in between.

Any individual can decide on an overall goal, purpose or mission, in trading for example. You can then set the intermediate goals, decide on and implement your overall strategy and the elements of your 'business plan', reviewing the opportunities to learn, change and grow on the way.

What are your beliefs and wishes, aspirations and goals from trading? Turn your planned and actual market experiences into pictures, or even vivid internal representations, through which you experience in your imagination what you will see, hear and feel when you have achieved your inevitable success.

In setting your goals, you may choose to optimise, rather than maximise your goals. Rewards involve some risk. The optimisation process in money management involves optimising the gains in the context of a chosen or managed level of risk. You could choose what risk you are prepared to accept before you begin. Through self-control, you can then optimise your performance in the context of that chosen limitation.

Don't bet the house if you can't afford to lose it. Many a poker player has lost everything by going beyond the 'bank' that they limited themselves to. Did you ever know someone who went to an auction and paid far more than they intended for the article they wanted. Set a limit and stick to it. Be prepared to walk away. If necessary, physically walk away. Leave the physical environment in which you are trading and go somewhere you can detach yourself, collect your thoughts, review your strategy and implementation, regroup and move forward.

The intermediate goals we set should be in keeping with the longer-term goals. They should be developmental or progressive. Sometimes, in achieving intermediate goals, we may go through a period where we may question everything that is happening and its possible effect on ultimate success. We are only a component of the market.

Through this book we may understand more about other people, as well as ourselves. It is often said that success at poker is based on psychology as much as probability. If we understand motivations and behaviours, we can take account of these.

Nevertheless, sometimes, things may not have gone according to plan. A major setback in the market might have caused us to review or even abandon a strategy for the time being. Console yourself that just as much money can be made from selling at a loss, buying back much cheaper and riding the gain back up again, as can be made in a rampant bull market. Setting, changing and accepting goals and objectives for your ultimate success involves parking your ego, making sound decisions, understanding and managing your behaviours and your self, achieving self-mastery.

Success at trading will have such a meaningful impact on so many aspects of your life, that it is a good idea to cross check your trading goals and maybe even integrate them with your interim life goals. Be relaxed and comfortable in yourself in the sure knowledge that your trading will not conflict with any other aspect of your life. You are at cause in everything and making objective choices in everything you do.

Setting and Visualising Outcomes

This process is described in the appendix. Once you have set your medium term goal, determine some event or outcome which will demonstrate to you beyond doubt that you have achieved this goal. Check the well formedness of the outcome, visualise it and put it out into your future. Determine and stick to your chosen trading style and strategy and entrust your future success to your unconscious mind. Be unsurprised when you may find yourself resetting your intermediate and longer-term goals even higher, as your success outstrips your previous expectations.

Continuous Improvement

The Japanese have a word 'kaizen' for the process of continuous improvement, used in TQM based organisations. This can be achieved by cycling through five questions:
- "What do I want to do? (Direction)
- What do I need to do it? (Resources)
- How am I going to do it? (Implementation)
- How am I doing? (Measurement)
- How can I improve what I am doing? (Improvement)."

(You can use the mnemonic - DRIMI).

In addition, you could apply the Cartesian questions earlier: what will I get, etc...

In summary, when you will have determined your goals, written them down and kept them under regular review, for continuous improvement, you may be delighted at the growing success you are achieving?

Trading and Investment Strategy.

"Trading is a mental and physical game which provides an intellectual , physical and emotional challenge of the highest order" (Rotella, *ibid.*).

There are innumerable trading styles and methodologies. Some of them work and some don't. But who is making the judgement? If you decided on a style to make a million dollars and only achieved $500,000, you might feel you had failed by your own standards. Most of us would be delighted!

The only trading or investment strategy which matters is your own - the one which is designed to achieve your goals. If it doesn't, you may want to be flexible enough to vary your strategy or even your goals. Of course, change your decisions with a specific purpose in mind. While there are many practical methods and techniques you might choose, depending on your chosen lifestyle and resources, some may be impracticable for you.

For example, if you wanted to successfully trade foreign currencies, you might have to take account of the fact that the major ones trade 'round the clock'. Would this fit with your preferred lifestyle and that of your stakeholders? Could you afford to be out of the market, or asleep when a critical point was reached?

You should have a carefully prepared game plan. Departing from it should only be the result of an equally well thought out decision. Too many players in the past have entered the market with a firm purpose and clearly defined rules, then departed from them when emotion took over. The depth of your emotional resources is as important as your finances. With inadequate emotional intelligence, a player might have quit in despair, or gambled more heavily than intended, as desperation struck and the purple mist blurred the vision.

When you have understood the source and character of your emotional responses to challenge and have learned how to minimise the negatives and enhance the positives, all the while remaining in control, then you are a winner.

Trading considerations

This is not a book about the detail of trading. You are or can become the master of those. The question is, will it take you months, or only weeks to be a master of yourself. Any amount of sound rationale and technique can be internalised - remember, you have only been using five percent of your brainpower. The world class poker player understands the plays, knows the probabilities inside out, can work out people, but above all, can remain calm and inwardly self-controlled, even under what others may find to be intense stress.

In tennis, there is a condition known as 'the elbow'. The pressures increased and the unfortunate player tightened up at the elbow. Suddenly, the shots that were scorching down the line, were being dumped into the net. The match was lost before they regained emotional control. At golf, one of the modern greats, Davis Love III has the 'cool' to walk away from the shot if his mind is not right, or his concentration disturbed. You can do the same, but first get the basics right.

The right brain is the domain of the emotions, the left of rational thought. You should be able to understand about the theory of efficient markets and the opportunities for arbitrage. All stock and money markets are risk based, and the processes of technical and fundamental analysis are ideal for improving your odds and the understanding of those markets. Following cycles for individual stocks and markets as a whole may indeed improve your percentages, as you spot the trends and breakouts. Computers do the same. To ignore them means taking unnecessary risk.

There are far too many players for you to ever dream of being the market. Despite his massive gains against sterling in the early 1990s, even George Soros' billions are not big enough to beat the market alone. Furthermore, as the big player emerges, the rest of the market watches their moves, following or backing against them as appropriate to the moment.

One way you can beat the market is to be yourself, with your own chosen strategy and a scale of play which is invisible to the rest of the players. If you can move the market on your own, you wouldn't need to read this book.

Now that you have your own clear game plan and you know the circumstances and the way you will depart from that if appropriate, under your own control, you can be resolved and remain unbiased, other than in favour of your own strategy. Part of that resolve is knowing when to be out of the market as well as when to be in. It takes just as much of your emotional strength to be clear in your belief that the market is in a bear trend, when it suddenly rises 1% in a day, as the result of a 'technical bounce' (temporarily oversold).

You will have your own script for trading. The style that you have developed will be yours and yours alone. Having used all the NLP techniques in this book, you understand yourself well. You have managed the changes you desired, achieved self-mastery in all aspects of your life, so that you never take a domestic 'situation' into the market. Your strategy and method fit you well and draw on your growing list of strengths which emerged as you have left the past behind.

You have experienced being 'in flow' when your unconscious mind made the calls and you knew afterwards that your conscious evaluation would prove the excellence of your judgement. You have eliminated the negatives from your internal dialogue, indeed some of it may be coming outside as the positive manifestations of your growing success spread through your optimistic outlook. Others around you have already noticed the change. In the markets like no-where else, people want to be around a winner. The only time a loser is a consolation, is when they've lost bigger than you did.

Being honest, for years I was probably a poor loser. I didn't think so, but I sure used to beat up on myself when things didn't go right. Since going through NLP training and taking on all these great psychological plays, I always go onto the course expecting to win. If I don't, I reflect on all the great shots I played and continue to practice my grooved technique. Most of all, I enjoy my own company now, as well as my playing partners. I shrug my shoulders and review where I can improve. I sustain my self-belief, quietly, in calm self-control - until the 30-foot putt drops!

Making the most of your game plan

So you have a game plan which you know is right for you. You work just as hard out of the market as you do inside it. By the time you go onto the course, you feel good, confident in your plays and the self-knowledge to know when to take a time out. Braggers and losers are not good to be around when the play didn't come off. And did you implement your stop loss.

Now you know how to play the percentage shot. Of course markets have setbacks, but the long-term trend is ever upwards. When you run your profits, ratcheting up your stop loss limit all the time, you are either making a bundle of money, or waiting out the fall to buy in cheaper.

Now you know who and where you are (your values, beliefs and positive expectations), you can confidently beat the averages, while many of the rest play hunches, ride their losses, become intense with the stress which merely becomes another challenge for you. You have seen your share of losers in the past and they kept on coming. Now you are above all that, the law of averages works in your favour. For every loser there is a winner - and you're it.

Your trading strategy is just like any other. Understand and improve the efficiency of your strategy, using the method in the 30-day programme. Remember it's not about the markets, it's about you.

You decide the strategy, you implement it. If it ever didn't work, it was the strategy you chose and designed. It was your responsibility if it ever didn't work out. It was your ability and self-mastery to stick to the chosen strategy, not depart. To recognise the need for refinement, take time out, adjust and implement the changes. If you ever lost control, played bigger than you intended, lost more than you could afford, it was you who decided the limits and did not implement them. Now that you are at cause in all that you do, have you already noticed the odds changing in your favour.

Just remember to reward yourself from time to time for your skill and self-mastery. And remember your stakeholders, who have their own emotional investment, while you have the control. Treat them to show how affluent you are becoming, while noticing how calm you can be and great to be around.

Volatility is a fact of life in the market. It is only a fact of life for you when you are in the market. Make it work for you and when it runs the other way, be content to sit dry on the bank, while the others take a bath.

One of the sayings of NLP is 'there is no content in content worth knowing'. The same is true of markets. There is no content for you, only context. You're invested in the market. Whether its going up or down is just context. If it's going up and you're in, you're happy. If its going down and you're out, you're very happy. You can change the context either by changing your perspective on the market, or by whether you're in or out.

When you've finished playing for the day, forget about it and go home. You cannot affect the market on your own. If you left yourself in overnight, that was your choice. If you stacked and walked away, there is another game tomorrow, with a different set of circumstances and more opportunities.

The optimum process in trading is the one that makes money. Unless you don't trade the market at all, you can often gain as much by minimising your losses as by maximising your gains. I don't mean panicking and bailing out, I mean implementing your strategy and staying out while the market falls. I mean using your limitless ability to work out the plays and going with the highest probability of winning average, rather than the lowest probability of winning huge. I never play the lottery and if I did, it would be just with 'fun money'.

When I play the markets, I have done the research, I have the system and the tools to support it. I know exactly the parameters on which I will deal. When I reach my target gain, or hit my stop loss, I walk away and leave it for someone else. I look for the next prospect. (In fact I always have more lined up, because the research never stops. In fact, sometimes a sale is dictated by my new target having hit the target buying price, as much as the old play reaching my peak).

Your problem solving, decision, trading and review processes are inextricably linked (see DRIMI, earlier). Now that you understand how you can fit your trading and money management processes to the best aspects of your personality, you can be your best. Ask yourself:
- What will I gain for myself when I win at trading?
- What will I have to give up when I win at trading?
- What would I get for myself by not trading?
- What would I have to forgo if I didn't trade?

And understand yourself and the insights you discovered, maybe for the first time?

You can have the self-mastery to sit out the market, missing the chance to trade and avoiding the losses that you might once have had to run, through those old worrying times. In the meantime, you can recharge your batteries and pay yourself a personal, as well as a financial dividend.

Once you have set and visualised your outcomes, be sure to reward yourself in the way you promised and foresaw. Anchor the great feelings of being a winner, over and over again and watch history repeat itself, now that you know you can be in control, as you choose.

Know when to go and know when to throw, is an old gambling saying. Money in the bank can earn money. Money in a static market has a time cost. When your stock was falling, you had to add two opportunity costs to your losses: the cost of money which could have been invested elsewhere and the cost of not being liquid to invest in the hotter prospect you had been rehearsing. Staying with the market is the same as buying the market. Make it a continuous conscious decision.

For many people, trading may be a nice little earner, but it's not a steady job. When you know you have the financial and emotional resources, you can change that. In the meantime, you can play to your own rules, in the market and in yourself, watching the pennies and the self-esteem grow.

Beware of confusing the fundamentals with the perceived fundamentals. When I was a stockbroker, someone once asked me "when is this market going to go up?". My reply was "when more people believe that than believe it will go down". Beware also, of people's expertise in predicting the past. Many an analyst or economist can explain to you lucidly why the market went down, but if they could always predict it, they wouldn't be doing their day job!

The market can never be right or wrong, because it always represents the total sum of the current decisions. The market is a natural process based on collective consciousness. It is subject to the laws of the universe. A market may appear irrational with regard to the fundamentals, but it is reflecting a collective set of behaviours. Run with the herd and get the herd's performance. Pay attention to the herd, choose your own strategy, implement it and stick to it, or make a rational change and watch yourself beat the herd. The question is, is your trading an occupation or a pastime? This will also help determine your method and strategy

The difference between trading and investment is time. Possible incidental loss is a probable incidence even of sound trading. Can you stay with the game? Losing streaks are opportunities to review and learn. An extended winning streak may once have produced the illusion of invincibility, leading to loss of everything. But no more.

You might start with an advantage if you start small and watch your self-confidence grow as your wealth does. Be affluent in spirit as well as in resource. Remember always to give back something of yourself and support those who do not have. The world is a big equation. When you give as well as receive, while you win, your world is in balance.

Chapter 4

What do you need to do it? - strategies for success

The Formula for Success.

Rotella's work (*ibid.*), while being excellent in many respects, had many negatives in it. Instilling fear in any way and to any degree, may work for someone who has an 'away from' set of values, or meta program. Who of us would not prefer to be motivated by positivity.

So how do I do that, some might say. The answer lies within and without, using the many tools and techniques described in this book, you may try in vain to recover any of those old patterns that you once ran, which used to hold you back.

It is true that to fulfil our limitless potential we can choose to unlearn any negative patterns of thought which we once had. These patterns had an emotional component. This component served to remind us from time to time that there had been an issue unresolved from our younger years. If we had ever gone into an unresourceful state, such as fear or panic as prices fell, what was the origin of that behaviour?

There was a positive lesson to be learned from that old memory. Our unconscious reminded us that the lesson had not been perceived or understood. Once we learned it, we could let go of the emotion and move forward in any aspect of our life that might previously have been affected.

In order to be as resourceful as we wish to be in our trading, we had to unlearn any negative patterns of behaviour. It was never necessary to be driven by fear to avoid a loss, when we can choose instead to be driven towards gain. That way we can use our unconscious programs to motivate our desire to succeed, running our gains, relying on our conscious, rationale to activate the stop loss if the price reverts.

For every trade, use the process of visualising outcomes to unconsciously programme your success. If, for any reason it is overtaken by circumstance, you can, in a wholly constructive and positive frame of mind, make a rational judgement that the game has changed and you will vary your strategy. When you do this through the process of self-mastery, your conscious and unconscious mind work in harmony to optimise your overall success.

Trading and not trading, making money and not making money, success and not success, for the time being, are all part of the rich pattern of the markets. Remember, you are not the market, just one component. You can choose to share in the success of appreciation and sit out the market or price correction, before your intuition tells you it is time to reinvest and your conscious thought processes confirm the fundamentals of your decision.

There are super-computers in use to predict and programme market investment and sale decisions. You do not need this sophistication. If you had billions of dollars of funds to invest, you could not afford to underperform the market. As a privateer, you can outperform the market on one factor alone: you can liquidate your entire portfolio if you wish. Also, the fund manager has to spread the risk and invest in the market components. With luck, they can outperform the average.

Meanwhile, statistics show that you do not need more than ten stocks in your portfolio at any one time. This sort of number gives you sufficient spread to largely insulate you from the disproportionate effect of one share on your portfolio. Meanwhile you can have sufficient concentration in the excellent investments you have made to outperform the market. Mix up growth shares with cyclicals bought at the right part of the cycle and you are well on your way.

Some say it is easier psychologically to buy than sell. However, there are different types of opportunity cost involved in each. If you are fully invested, you may restrict your flexibility to seize the opportunity which presents itself, not being able to buy when the time is right. Out of the market, there is the opportunity cost involved in the performance of the shares you might otherwise be invested in. Some may say that you cannot lose money if you are out of the market. Others say you cannot make money, either. Decide what is right for you.

There are two ways to 'go a bear' of the market. One is to sell shares in the hope of buying back in cheaper. The other is to wait in the first place for the right opportunity to buy. Whichever approach you choose should be right for you, in the context of your overall strategy. Apart from the rules and regulations of dealing and investment, the market is an unstructured environment, so set your own rules and structure in a way that controls and limits complexity. Keep it simple!

Frustration in life may in the past have occurred through not knowing, not being in control, rather than failure or disappointment. It can be one aspect of human nature to seek resolution. Trading, like life, creates more questions than answers.

NLP based therapies produce lasting, fundamental resolution and success. A trainer was once asked "you have been using these techniques for ten years - you must have resolved every problem you ever had?" The reply was "life can be like a road...you go down a road to the end...and there's another opportunity.

Trading can be a road to self-discovery, creating riches in life, as well as wealth

Don't try to beat the market because you may end up by beating yourself. Golf is like trading. If you cheat, you are cheating yourself. When, on the other hand, you are being the best you can be...or better, you set the rules for your own success. Nothing else matters. You are at cause in the market and in your life. It cannot make you do anything which you do not choose to do.

Using a mechanical approach alone, dictated by the rules you have laid down and rigidly applied, misses the possibilities of your intuition. In my own experience, I have used fundamental and technical analysis to underwrite or correct my own judgement. We are all connected to the universal conscious and as we open our minds, there are infinite possibilities. The chances for gain must be as numerous as those for loss for this universe to be in balance.

If you toss a penny 100 times, the probability is that it will come down heads 50 times. This doesn't often happen in practice, because chance intervenes. If it has come down 100 times consecutively as a head, there is still an even chance it will come down a head next time. You can use more science and more art in investment and trading. The art is to know instinctively when to trade. The science is to know how to use the fundamentals to avoid the obvious pitfalls which may already exist in the market.

Intuition may suggest I buy Wal-Mart shares. Fundamentals can tell me to avoid them if the company has just published a forecast downturn in sales. It may be a sound investment, and there may be a better time to buy.

In the UK, we talk of penny shares. When a company is written up in the press, the small investor tries to buy, but the market maker marks up the shares. Disproportionate gains can be seen in one day. Many small investors still buy, for fear of missing out. Eventually the market settles down. There are no more buyers. The shares fall back and I can buy on sound fundamentals, knowing that there should not be many sellers, because penny share investors tend to run their losses.

Use mechanical systems and fundamentals to augment your judgement. Find a system which suits your own make-up so that art and science can be in harmony. It is good to understand market psychology and make it work for you. Understanding your own is even better.

Success factors

"We all have purposes that drive us...wherever we see people succeeding, the same factors seem to appear time and time again... We always find, for instance, a drive, enthusiasm or passion... We find strong beliefs...beliefs about yourself, what you are capable of doing... And linked with these, there is usually a strong system of values... We also notice that successful people, as well as knowing where they want to be, usually seem to follow some plan or strategy... They seem organised in their thinking and the way they marshal internal and external resources... They also seem to have a certain energy - not just physical strength and fitness, but an inner energy that keeps them going against all the odds when ordinary people would have given up." (*NLP*, Dr Harry Alder, Piatkus, 1994).

The above book was one of the earliest on NLP to be published in the UK. In it, Dr Alder identifies four steps to success in any situation: know what you want (know your outcome); take action; learn to notice the results of what you do; be prepared to change your behaviour until you get the result you are after.

Whether reading Sun Tzu's thoughts on the art of war, Zen Buddhism or chaos theory, you may come to the same conclusion on the value of counter-logic and the value of following your own intuition and instinct, rather than the herd.

From quantum physics, we understand that a particle moves as a result of being observed. Schrodinger's puzzle is whether a cat put into a box with a radioactive isotope has died. If we open the box some time after, finding the cat dead, how do we now when it died, or whether indeed it was us opening the box and observing it that caused it to die.

If we keep watching the markets, or a particular price because we are preoccupied with a possible negative outcome, how do we know if it occurs whether it was a result of our act of observation. My wife visualises car parking spaces in a busy town and they persistently appear. Ever since I set my mission and goals and visualised the outcomes, my 'luck' has changed dramatically, with wonderful consequences...

In his wonderful books 'Creating Affluence' and 'The Seven Spiritual Laws of Success', Deepak Chopra also writes of limitless potential:

"Inherent in every intention and desire is the mechanics for its fulfilment...intention and desire in the field of pure potentiality have infinite organising power. And when we introduce an intention in the fertile ground of pure potentiality, we put this infinite organising power to work for us." And

"Therefore you have the ability to acquire anything that falls within the realm of your imagination, and even those things that are currently outside the limits of your imagination. The more you acquire, the more your imagination will expand. What is unimaginable today might become imaginable tomorrow."

Whether in trading or in life in general, we are on a road of continuous learning, improvement, personal growth and self-discovery. It does not take much to become an expert in a particular field. As someone once said, all you need to do to become a millionaire is to know a bit more than anyone else about one subject.

If you traded the markets in ignorance, you may have got unexpected results. When you have invested the time and effort to understand as much as you need to know, on an ongoing basis, you can move towards limitless success. At the very least you will overlook the pitfalls of blind speculation.

Learn speed-reading and read as much as possible. Lateral thinking comes from the integration of right and left brain processes.

Intuition also comes from the right brain. For too long we may have let left brain thinking dominate our daily activities. By all means use logical and rational thought. Where do inspiration and insight spring from - inside? If you want average performance, settle for average thinking. It is the extraordinary thought which comes from intuition partnered with judgement, which can inspire your success.

Some years ago, I became very ill. Eventually it was realised that my immune system had all but collapsed, under self-imposed stress. As I realised this, I began to get better and put in place irreversible changes which are producing great positive results in my life. Part of my journey, was to experience, understand and then acquire the tools and techniques of NLP based therapies. Another step was to minimise left-brained activity for a period and focus wholly on the right brain.

I wrote poetry and music, painted and read. It restored nature's balance. We all have the skills of intuition and insight. Find them in yourself. Make them work for you or settle for the average. Do what you have always done and get what you always got. Follow the herd and get average performance, or worse. The Dow theory of markets suggests that when everyone is jumping from the buildings, that is the time to buy. When they are buying as if there is no tomorrow, consider selling.

There are any number of sayings in life which are applied to the market; 'cut your losses and let your profits run; you won't go broke taking a profit; always leave something for the next person; s(he) who fights and runs away lives to fight another day'; etc.

Learn to understand the important difference between speculation and gambling. 'Speculate to accumulate'...

In trading, there are few substitutes for motivation, commitment and focus. Environment and surroundings are critical. Add to these the power of the many techniques you will have understood from this book and watch your success multiply. Transport your environment, if necessary. You can do this with anchors, for example, which fill you with a hugely positive state recalled from music, rewards, or whatever works for you

Self-Mastery

The key to success in trading is self-mastery. Too often, in life, in sport, in business and especially in trading, the ego got in the way. Too often in business and in the markets, have I seen someone come to grief, when their ego got too big. Gerald Ratner built a successful business. At a business lunch, he proudly stated "we sell c**p". Ratner's shares plummeted, he resigned, and the company (once the biggest jewellers in the UK) had to change its name to Signet to rebuild its brand.

I say again - no one person is bigger than the market they trade in. By all means celebrate your wins and remember the law of averages. It will take continuing commitment, diligent preparation, hard work and self-control to stay ahead. How many people did you ever hear of, who, having had a big win at anything, ended up losing the lot and more.

Rotella (*ibid.*) lists 'thirteen important character traits some of the better traders possess'. Match this list to the techniques for self-mastery in this book:

- Self control;
- Accepting responsibility for actions;
- Operating in an unstructured environment
- Thinking independently and creatively;
- Willingness to take risks and accept losses;
- Inability to control and comprehend the market
- Ability to adapt to constant change;
- Ability to act on your decisions;
- Ability to withstand stress;
- Emotional detachment;
- Patience;

- Enthusiasm, commitment and focus;
- Self-direction.

And note all the ways in which you are already changing and implementing these on a daily basis. Maybe you have already acquired the qualities of self control through self mastery, learning and growing each day... Know yourself, seek to continuously improve as a key part of self mastery.

As Daniel Goleman says in '*Working with Emotional Intelligence*' (Bloomsbury 1998): "Emotional intelligence skills are synergistic with cognitive ones; top performers have both. The more complex the job, the more emotional intelligence matters - if only because a deficiency in these abilities can hinder the use of whatever technical expertise or intellect a person may have."

Emotional awareness is "The recognition of how our emotions affect our performance and the ability to use our values to guide our decision making". And, having made our values predominantly positive, in how many ways are you already seeing success in your trading and indeed your life?

Finally, Goleman says people with self-control "manage their impulsive feelings and distressing emotions well; stay composed, positive and unflappable even in trying moments; think clearly and stay focused under pressure."

With objective self-knowledge, an understanding of your strengths and opportunities for improvement, insight and intuition, the proper mindset and a willingness to change and grow, you can transform your trading prospects..

Struggle in trading was a state we created only in ourselves. Stress is a product of growing demands tapping into old unwanted states. Use the techniques in the 30-day programme to remove those states and old redundant beliefs and stress have become a thing of the past. The old, unresourceful traits and emotional states which may have been present in everyday life, may have contradicted those needed for optimal trading. This is the point of self-mastery

I have found much contemplation and personal growth from reading The Tao. It will be a constant reference source throughout my life. I have found such inner peace and calmness since.

"When I let go of what I am, I become what I might be. When I let go of what I have, I receive what I need....and,

To know how other people behave takes intelligence, but to know myself takes wisdom." (Both quotes from *The Tao of Leadership*, John Heider, Gower 1992).

You and you alone are responsible for your actions and of their implementation. From the Tao and other works, we understand the importance focus and the subjugation of self. Those who end up believing they might walk on water, somehow seemed to drown. If you can keep your head when those around you...

Strategies

Now that you have developed your own trading strategy and methodology, you need to be sure that your style and implementation are all your own. It is fundamental that your personal implementation strategy fits with your personality and that your chosen trading strategy fits your everyday strategy.

For example, everyone has a decision strategy for anything. It is preceded by a motivation strategy, and is followed by a convincer strategy and a reassurance strategy. Indeed, we have a strategy for everything from living and learning to loving. The unconscious strategy you used to select your partner may be broadly similar to that which you use to buy a car, or to open a trade.

Review the section on rep systems at the back of the book and try these...how did you know it was time to buy that stock? Did you see something, hear something or feel something? Run the movie from start to finish, observing what is happening in your internal representations (what you see, hear or feel). Write down the apparent pattern. Does it seem logical? Is anything apparently missing, or out of order, such that you can improve this strategy?

Decision strategies are at the core of all of our actions. Many of us run what are called 'synesthesias'. The clues are often in the words, or the actions, e.g. 'it grabbed my eye' (KV, kinaesthetic/ visual synesthesia), or 'I saw it and bought it' (there is probably a K in between, because presumable we have a feeling about something just before we decide). Imagine if you traded with this pattern. You might buy or sell on hunch the whole time. How far would that be removed from gambling?

When we buy or sell something, we may also run a strategy that is to do with being convinced that we did the right thing (a convincer strategy). So you bought the watch. How long was it before you were convinced it was the right decision? Did you know immediately? Did you need to ask some other people? Do you have to look at it every day to be sure?

How do you know someone is good at their job? Do you have to see, hear or feel something? How many times do you need this evidence before you are convinced, or do you need constant evidence? If the latter, will you ever be reassured? What would have happened if you had run a constant convincer strategy for your trading? Might you have been in constant self-doubt about whether you had made the right decision? On the other hand, if you were automatically convinced, how many bad trades might you have made? Maybe a little fundamental evidence to augment your decision would be a good thing.

So, having elicited your own strategy and checked it out for trading, would it be good to put some constructive self-talk in there somewhere, to ask inside "is this the right decision? What evidence is there to confirm my decision?" Only once may be enough, because this is confirmation and getting your conscious and unconscious mind working in harmony, until it becomes second nature. When you buy something in the shops, do you ever find yourself taking it back? When you buy through the Internet, have you ever made a decision you regretted (buyer's remorse).

What positive change could you make to any of your strategies which will improve your percentages in trading and life, for that matter?

Any successful strategy should be created, tested, constantly applied, and kept under objective review. Your learning strategy is pretty important to your life and trading. How do you learn best and how can you ensure you go on learning? What check is built into your processing, which reviews your decisions, looking for ways to improve your performance?

Language and internal dialogue

Did you ever know anyone who used to beat themselves up if things didn't work out? When they spoke of a new initiative, or were practically or implicitly challenged, was there negativity in their response, or their self-talk? We have covered limiting beliefs elsewhere, but your everyday language is not only important for your positive state of mind, it is also a window into your innermost feelings and the programs and patterns you run.

After I recovered from illness, I got up one morning and was planning my day. I heard myself say " today I must do …and I've got to do …and yesterday I should have done …so I'll have to do it today… My language was full of imperatives. We call them modal operators of necessity (MONS).

These are OK in the right situation for you. So, if you cannot buy the stock when your call option expires, you must close the trade. A safety engineer must follow the rules. A nuclear physicist must take all the right precautions for public safety, etc.

So I asked myself what I was going to do about it. Replace them with choices. So, I would like to do…and I could do…and I can do …and I want to do …and I will do …These were modal operators of possibility (MOPS) for possibility, options and choices.

Use MOPS and MONS as you see or feel to be appropriate. You might decide to use MONS for method, strategy or implementation. Make it your own decision. If anyone else makes those decisions for you, be sure you understand it is your choice to implement them. If you have ever said to yourself "I cannot..." about anything, did you already understand that this is a MOP - I can do the process of not... So now are you seeing things with more possibilities?

Financial and Emotional Resources

If you ever experienced losing money while trading, did it draw on your emotional as well as financial resources? Why was that? What was it from your past which was associated by your unconscious mind to that experience?

When I was young, money was tight. I remember once losing my holiday spending money that I had saved up for weeks and being distraught. This left a pattern which was reinforced when my father's investment money went the same way. I felt responsible, even guilty. When I later came to trade on my own behalf, I would grab a profit while it was there and watch a loss like a rabbit in the headlights of a car.

How did I change that? First, by accessing the originating emotional experience, learning the message that my unconscious mind had carried for so long, putting the whole experience in a new, rational context and letting go of the emotions. I then worked on fear of failure, releasing this unresourceful emotion. Adding in highly positive motivational tools, such as powerful positive anchors and changing strategies, so that reflection was introduced, I am now much more relaxed and calm when trading. Indeed, I positively enjoy it - especially making money.

Drawdown is a critical factor, whether you are trading or playing poker. If you traded beyond your means, you may have run the risk of losing everything. It is possible that you had broken your own trading rules or limits, or maybe they were too loose or non-existent in the first place.

By all means consciously trade with the understanding that you may lose all of the stake money you have decided you can afford to lose. Forty years ago, my father won over £1,000 on horse racing. This was a huge amount for a man earning only £20 a week at the time. Being a generous man, he took us to London and bought us all a new outfit. My mother got a fur coat. Then he set aside £500 and played with the remainder. He had won it and he decided he could afford to lose it. It worried my mother for years because of the amounts involved, but he got 30 years of pleasure out of his windfall by sticking to a system that had worked so well in the first place.

When you have understood yourself, released the negative emotions from the past, made the positive changes in your patterns of behaviour and your life and put yourself at cause, you will have much greater emotional drawdown. This will enable you to always be in control, balancing intuition with rational thinking, without being overtaken by any old pattern which you may once have run. And have you noticed that your financial drawdown holds up better too?

You make the choices, so rely on yourself. The market will still be there tomorrow. When you have evolved clear trading and personal strategies, focussed your attention on the matter in hand, put the old outside pressures completely outside yourself, answered to yourself alone (because you are in control), you may find both the success and enjoyment of trading are growing. The financial and the emotional entry costs have become much lower, you have access to internal, as well as external information at will. You can assess the position calmly and with complete self-mastery, didn't you?

Some writers consider the risk of ruin. Why would you ever need to have considered that when you plan to be successful and both your trading and personal strategies are in harmony. Who on earth would want to visualise failure or total loss? When the last thing you thought about before hitting the ball was whether it would go out of bounds, did the muscles tense up and produce the shot you feared? Visualise your continuing success and, having cleared your mind of whatever irrational fears that may have existed, implement your winning plan.

Who would choose to be motivated by the fear of failure, or the risk of ruin? If you knew someone like that, how would they have stopped the negative patterns creeping in? Do you want to enjoy your trading and your life - yes! Money is a limitless commodity because we keep printing more of it as we need it. Inflation ensures that the stock of money continues to grow. Even average performance implies an increase in worth.

Just one word of caution. It is good to have a rational awareness of the possibility of a market crash. This is yet another reason for not always trading at the limit of one's financial resources. Even the best of investors has in the past been taken unawares by the rapidity of change, such as 'Black Monday'. I was out of the market in 1987, but even when I have been exposed at times of other sharp falls, there was always something kept back which was used to buy in at lower levels. Apart from 1929, the prices of quality stocks have tended to rebound quite quickly.

Gambling, speculation and entertainment can be a costly business, if they involve too high a proportion of your core resources. By all means enjoy yourself, and make it a conscious choice, shared with the stakeholders in your life. From the Tao to Deepak Chopra, many philosophers in history have stressed the importance of giving something back, to keep things in balance. This is especially so in donating a steady and reasonable proportion of your gains to charity and needy causes. It helps those who cannot help themselves and it is good for the spirit. (And keep it to yourself, otherwise it demeans your motives).

Keep a healthy perspective on markets at all times. Gamblers all over the world have been susceptible to being drawn into the pervading view, or someone else's hunch, desperate for a win. By all means run with the herd, while keeping a detached overall perspective and being selective in your view. If you persistently adopt someone else's view, expect their performance. In that case, why don't you just put the money into one of the thousands of funds and crystallise your implicit delegation of responsibility. (Or was it ever abdication of choice?)

By all means be optimistic in business and in trading and temper this with realism and pragmatism. You will already have realised that underpinning the whole philosophy of this book is positivism and being your best in all things. The market is a microcosm of life-it is the sum total of all human emotions. There is more than enough negativism and misery around, so collect more than your share of enjoyment and the positive and watch your fortunes grow. Have vision, resilience and endurance to achieve unlimited success.

I have heard and read so many people analogise the markets with battles and wars. Is this how you want to trade, or be in life in general. Save these emotions for computer games and chess. If you choose to see markets as battles and life as war, at least understand the wisdom and calmness of Sun Tzu. By all means use the cunning of Machiavelli if you wish, but leave out the meanness of spirit.

If you were ever mean or bitter, those emotions were happening inside you. Any virus infection you had in the past, unleashed the war machine in your blood cells. Do you recall what that felt like on the worst days? Why would you ever have wanted your positive, loving mind to be infected by mean thoughts?

If we ever fought battles, the main opponent was ourselves. If any sport ever became a battle, did it enhance your performance?

It may have unleashed your adrenaline or your drive and determination, but what great commander in history was without compassion.

Relax. Use moments between trades and time away from the markets to recharge your batteries and invest in reviewing and updating your technical and fundamental information. Give as much care to your emotional and your financial resources.

Chapter 5

How are you going to do it? - positive language and behaviour

We have considered many practicalities of trading as you have moved forward with this book. It is a horizon of new choices. You may already have noticed the balance is changing, as the self-development aspects grow. Now that you are understanding so many positive and constructive things about yourself and as you try out all the fascinating tools and techniques, in how many ways is your trading changing for the better. How many new opportunities are opening up for you. How many new insights do you have, including into other players?

We have talked of character traits. These are exhibited most clearly in language and behaviour. The key was to eliminate any old negative patterns you may have had, invest in and progressively grow the positives. Weed out the underperformers you have no use for and invest in the growth aspects of your personality.

As a therapist, the model I use is one of supply and demand. Executives are referred to me 'suffering from stress'. Any good counsellor will facilitate the environment in which the client recognises any stress triggers which may have been present and progressively eliminates or rationalises them. This is what I call the demand side of stress management.

Using NLP based therapies, I guide the client back to the source of the unresourceful behaviours. In the absence of trauma, these are almost exclusively in the first twenty-one years of their life -

often the first ten. When they have reviewed the source of original emotional distress or conflict which led to a state being triggered and were able to put in a constructive perspective, they let go of the emotion. Retaining the learnings, they moved forward having eliminated the real source of stress. This I call the supply side. Once this is rationalised stress can cease to be a problem.

Karma, or peace, achieved through meditation and self-mastery can be just as important in remaining in control of your ability to fulfil your potential as a trader.

The Relevance of Presuppositions

In chapter two, when we were considering filters, we reviewed the presuppositions inherent in NLP. In the later section on Strategies, we considered Rotella's list of desirable character traits for success in the markets. Below, I have related these to the presuppositions. Take a moment to review these, realising already how your unconscious mind has understood and begun to synthesise these into your life and trading.

- Self control = sell mastery/choice/rules (H)
- Accept responsibility (a,c,g,e,h)
- Ability to function in unstructured inbound (I,n)
- Ability to think independently and creatively (n,c)
- Willingness to accept risk and take losses (g)
- Accepting your inability to control and comprehend everything in the market (c,I,l,n)
- Ability to adapt quickly to constant change environment (l)
- Ability to act on your decision (h)
- Ability to withstand stress (a,g,h, I,j,l)
- Emotional detachment (a,b)
- Patience (g,l)
- Enthusiasm, commitment and focus
- Self direction

In addition, with regard to your trading, take a piece of paper, quarter it and ask yourself these four questions:

- What am I good at?
- What do I enjoy doing?
- What is successful and makes money?
- What fits with my mission and overall goals?

See what appears. Check off only those things that appear in all four lists. Change your life as necessary to you for the purpose of fulfilling your potential and desires. I did this exercise and the following list developed:

- Leading change, personal growth and transition for individuals and teams;
- Working with individuals to eliminate behaviours and language that used to hold them back (including coaching, counselling and therapy where appropriate), facilitating the release of their limitless potential;
- Public presentations of NLP based personal development;
- Trading the stock market successfully;
- Writing books on personal growth and right brain topics;
- Composing music, painting and reading.

Only five years ago, I was pursuing a very left brained career path. I had refused to listen to the internal voice which tried to tell me I had been unhappy in myself for years. I had not spotted that, despite a highly successful career in financial services, I had changed every role from left-brained finance and process management into right brained creativity and people management. I had been complimented for writing well (and quickly) and speaking persuasively (even occasionally with charisma). I left too little time for myself, my stakeholders, relaxation and recharging the batteries. The rest, as they say, is history.

I am now happier, calmer, more resourceful and at peace with myself than in my whole previous life. I invest 10% of my time giving to young people the opportunity for change before unresourceful patterns have established themselves. When I understood the potential of NLP for positive change, saw and felt the results in myself, I was prepared to respond to almost any request to help others to grow in the way I had - especially at a younger age.

Oh and by the way, I have reduced my golf handicap by 10 shots and it will fall another 10 in the next year, applying similar techniques, positive attitudes and thought processes those I am sharing with you now.

Competencies, Strengths and Opportunities for Improvement

In a competitive world, many more organisations are doing an audit of competencies. Apart from helping to place round pegs in round holes, it more importantly identifies people with potential for growth. Both the organisation and the individual need to continue to grow, adapt and evolve, in order to keep pace with the game.

As individuals, we have a set of competencies for every aspect of our lives. We can develop new ones as well as enhancing the existing. A presupposition of NLP is that if one person can do something excellently well, another can learn to do it. We all use similar combinations of thought and muscular movements. Even the ape has over 95% of the same genes as us humans.

When you can believe in your limitless potential and the ability to change and grow continuously, then trading gives you the opportunity to see yourself as you can be.

Every experience in trading, as in life, is an opportunity to learn. What is the message inherent in the new or changed situation?

Some talk of strengths and weaknesses. I see what are described as weaknesses by some, as undeveloped opportunities. Among those we are now growing are insight and intuition. Insight is literally looking within to find an answer. When we restricted ourselves to conscious thought, we used only 5% of our mind's potential.

Through study of Eastern philosophy, many Westerners have sought the path to the higher self. Don Juan tried mind altering drugs. Our minds are part of a greater consciousness. The paths we are beginning to tread are old paths that we lost thousands of years before.

Intuition lies within the unconscious. It literally means inner learning. This and the other specific traits to optimise your trading are a function of your beliefs and your emotional state at the time. As you opened your mind to limitless possibilities and cleared the emotional blocks from the way, did you not begin to see the skills you already possessed? What is your desired trait-set, so that you are in control of your trading and can be your very best? Having identified and closed the gaps, you can then see the whole. You can learn character traits or understand or change what's already within you.

A singular mindset could work against you. Stubbornness and single mindedness may have produced results for you in the past, and how many opportunities did you overlook in the process? Your unconscious mind records and remembers everything. Once you have found the way to tap into the void, where all understanding lies, then you can change anything that hasn't worked for you in the past.

Understand, for example, the source of your emotions, enhance the positives, change or remove the negatives, change or remove your limiting beliefs.

Representation systems

We all have a set of representation systems, which are part of our unique make-up. Each individual may have a primary or dominant representation system which biases the filtering process. The rep systems are: visual, auditory, kinaesthetic (including physical and emotional feeling), olfactory and gustatory. Every experience you have, or memory you have stored uses one or more of these. The more we use to store a memory, the stronger it may be.

Use all your senses when you are assessing a market opportunity or trading - look, see, hear, feel, smell and taste what is going on. I teach dyslexics how to read, spell, or write. Very often they were running an inefficient strategy, such as trying to spell through their feelings. A fifteen-year-old boy learned how to read and spell properly in just two hours. Can you imagine how many new choices open up for you when you have a similar experience?

Learn to trade the markets by touch, as athletes and sports people do, finding their way into 'the zone', where they can be in 'flow'.

Insight has another connotation, for we can all make internal representations, especially pictures. When you have visualised a future memory, seen, felt and heard all that will happen, through your own eyes and internal senses, stepped out of the picture and put it out into your timeline, think of the limitless opportunities you can create. Look within yourself and see yourself as you really are, in your most positive light, or better still, as you really can be.

Nobody makes you do or feel anything. We do it ourselves. Understand that and change any unresourceful state to positive.

Some see trading as a game of winners and losers. Winning and losing are an attitude created inside our own minds. Both are the consequences of our attitudes and beliefs and the steps we took. Remember the law of requisite variety - the person who is most capable of adapting to change will end up controlling the system, for themselves and in their own set of beliefs. When you have set out the goals, the rules, the strategy and the method; when you see yourself as you really are and see everything as an opportunity which only you can choose for yourself, then you will fulfil your trading potential. Start now...yes, right now!

Language & Behaviours

NLP is fundamentally about how we language and behave. When I was young, I thought I had discovered an original thought, when I postulated that everybody else might be the product of my imagination (or I theirs). Later I found many others had come to the same conclusion. It is part of awareness of self and beingness.

Rene Descartes said 'I think, therefore I am'. Chomsky invented eprime, the English language without any conjugation of the word 'to be'. Now, I realise that everything in the world is a product of my own mind. If anything doesn't happen as a representation inside me, then it doesn't happen for me.

When I do not believe in, or cannot create the state of losing in my mind, it does not happen for me. The mind is so clever and so powerful that we can create internal experiences so vivid that we cannot tell the difference between imagination and reality (hence 'mind-altering' drugs). When you have used the combination of techniques in this book to remove unresourceful behaviours and limiting beliefs, replacing them with limitless potential and positivity, there is no limit to what you can achieve.

Everything we do is represented in language and behaviours. Consciously or unconsciously we can represent and store every experience in models constructed in language. For example, the word sad, for me, conjures up a unique collection of memories and feelings, conscious and unconscious. Some people have worked on stripping away the structure of language from clients' experience and memory. Eventually they get to deep-seated emotions and 'prime concerns'.

NLP compares the surface structure of language and behaviour with the deep structure. 'The map is not the territory. (The surface representation is not the whole person, we are always much more than that). However, in some senses the map is the territory. What the therapist, the client and each of us experience at the surface may often be the only clues to what is really going on deep inside. 'Where did that state come from'?

In NLP, Bandler and Grinder analysed language and constructed the 'Meta model' which others have taken forward. There are now at least 60 subdivisions of the Meta model, which can be discerned in the language patterns of the individual to give insights into the unique patterning of their deep structure. For example, some people are driven away from failure, while others drive themselves towards success. Offer the former a bonus or beat the latter with a stick and you may not get the response you expect, depending on your own patterning. The Meta model questions at the end will help you discern some of your own and others most important patterns.

We discussed MOPS and MONS earlier and the possible positive changes you are already making. Many people have had an internal voice, or internal dialogue. This is called auditory digital and is catalogued alongside the other rep systems.

If you have ever had internal dialogue, how did it speak to you, or how did it behave? Did you ever come across someone who experienced the 'inner saboteur'? This was the voice that crept in to make someone irrationally frightened, guilty, jealous or whatever, when there was absolutely no need to be. It came from old patterns that were based on 'all good things must come to an end' and similar negative and self-destructive programs.

We shall come back to rep systems, when we have understood the power of submodalities to 'describe' our inner representations and especially as a medium for lasting change. In the meantime, understand the power of language.

As you visualise new opportunities and choices in your trading, make them bigger, bolder, brighter and more powerful inside. Add in the infinite potential of empowering, positive language and you may already be noticing the many ways in which you are changing.

How do you describe yourself to yourself? "I am a great trader, who uses a combination of great technical and professional skill, together with intuition, insight, vision and creativity to produce success beyond what I might once have believed possible..."

Deciding with Conviction

Now you have understood the importance of language, you see the value of being clear in what you plan to achieve and deciding with positive conviction. It is importance to trust in the system you have decided on, because by now it has come from the best of you. Believe in your self and you are the system, for all your purposes when you take it on.

By all means also apply the basic techniques of risk management:

- What is the problem?
- What are the possible courses of action?
- What are the likely consequences of implementation?
- What are the probabilities which attach?
- Which of the courses will minimise your risk of loss?
- Which will optimise your prospects of gain, at an understood level of risk?
- When you review the decision process, is there any way you can improve?
- Is there anything which you might not do, or stop doing, to improve prospects?

Make your decisions based on sound judgement; act on them; follow through with them; live with any consequences, including executing decisions to buy or sell according to a predetermined plan (e.g. implementing stop losses).

You can do any amount of analysis, and eventually you will want to make a decision, including the possibility of doing nothing (providing it is an active, not a passive decision). You may seek the advice of others, read or otherwise study information relevant to the decision - absorb it all and then listen to the calm voice of reason inside you.

Brokers and other advisors cannot always be impartial and objective. Even if they are legally obliged to state an interest in a particular investment (including, e.g. 'we are buying this stock for other clients' or 'we act for this company'), there may be other considerations.

My own broker is a good friend, who has given me some good tips. One of these I had bought at £1, held up to £1.30 and then sold on a stop loss limit when the market fell badly. It rose rapidly to £5 before I had a chance to get back in and was written up by the brokers to the company as being worth £8.

Within weeks, the market fell again from 6,500 to 4,800. On the day it bottomed out, this share was one of my selections, at £1.92. I rang my friend. The market had fallen seriously that day. I asked him his views. He said he would have real concerns about buying anything before we had seen a confirmed recovery. I bought the shares on my own firm conviction and they now stand at £12.

By all means seek advice, but always make up your own mind. Base your decisions on a mix of intuition and fundamentals. Open your mind to all possibilities. As you are becoming more confident in your judgement and choices and calmer in yourself, you can see the benefits almost daily. As you make the choices in your own life and trading, you are responsible for the consequences and can be open to the learnings.

Whether you enter, exit or even stay out altogether is your call. There has never been any compulsion either way, unless of course you knew someone who was a gambler. When the next fix of adrenaline has driven decisions, then luck was a commodity of real relevance. Make your own luck by better and better daily practice. Find in yourself the ability to remain 'cool under fire'. Discover, build and enjoy your own karma.

The market is a mass psychology, as well as increasingly a set of mathematical models. The models are increasingly correcting and smoothing volatility (eliminating arbitrage). All that matters is that you are aware when your own evaluation of the market or a subject is correct for you, in the context of your chosen plan, strategy and methodology.

Trading Style and Mentality

Trading is a game of probability. Traders must be calm and detached from other than the sheer pleasure of success and growing self-confidence and self-esteem at a job well done. And that's what it is. I trade the markets for fun now, with a limited 'bank' and only when I have the time for uninterrupted focus and concentration.

There is something about us when our left and right brain are in perfect harmony. For me it is the ability to see a picture of the opportunity, to know instinctively that this is the right opportunity. Maybe all the information I have absorbed means that my unconscious mind is alert and watching for the chance.

Like when I was eleven and picking the horse for my Dad. I knew little about statistics and even less about horse racing. Yet, somehow, when I lay on the floor reviewing the previous day's results and making today's selections, my mind must have been drawing on that hidden database to consistently make good choices. Between the left and the right, I was making the right connections and the analysis was unconscious and automatic.

How to Develop the Optimal Trading Method and Mentality

What matters is the method that is right for you and having a wholly positive approach. If you have researched a company, the fundamentals are sound and the market as a whole is not in a bear phase, a fall in the price of the stock you just bought is making it an even better proposition. How few companies actually go bust? Some say you cannot plan for profit warnings, but a good and careful reading of the accounts, an understanding of the sector, competitors and the important market factors, all contribute. Always keep in mind an opinion about the management themselves. Do they have a track record of success, here or elsewhere?

Develop a trading style which is all your own. There are many examples and models to choose from. It should fit you like a glove. The closer it feels to your own personality and philosophy, the more instinctive you can become in implementing it.

My father followed a racehorse tipster called Mr X, who specialised in picking three outsiders every day. He then backed them in each way doubles and one treble. He was very successful for three years. Meanwhile, my Dad realised that Mr X would have a long losing streak after a big win. He wasn't a wealthy man. So, he adapted his own plan, staying out for ten days after a win and then building up the stake. That was his own style and method and that's how he won £1,000.

It goes without saying that the ideal trading mentality is positive, optimistic and focused. It is based around taking personal responsibility for every decision made, in an objective way, based on the chosen strategy and method. Whether you go for large or small profits, or whatever method you use, it is important to keep a record of your results. You then have the chance to review the method objectively and adjust it accordingly. It is true that different methods will work better or worse at different times.

Suppose you are trading in high volatility stocks, such as Internet companies or 'hi-tech'. If the market itself is in a quiet phase, such as the summer break, you may not make any money. If you understand the market and its phases, you can change your strategy or method accordingly.

When I sold out in July 1987, it was because of concerns about junk bonds. With the situation unresolved, when I cautiously re-entered the market at the sharply lower levels in November, I weighted more heavily to utilities and supermarkets, based on their resilience in difficult markets. As the trends of recovery were confirmed, I increased the weighting of high beta stocks and reduced the 'safe' stocks.

We considered optimisation earlier. If you go for maximisation of profits you may strike lucky. Who around you can consistently call the top, however. Optimisation means maximising your gains at a managed level of risk. It means eliminating as far as possible the risk of loss and having a set of criteria that understands and takes account of the risks you have estimated. Your risk-adjusted gains may not individually match the best in the market, but you may find you consistently perform better with your whole portfolio over time.

This is my own view. What matters for you is yours and what fits with and is right for you. Then you can trade on instinct and professionalism.

The question may become are you prepared to change to a system that works, or are you going to modify that system to fit your personality and style? It's like dating. Are you going to go with anyone and risk the consequences, or are you going to use more science and listen to your intuition, knowing instinctively who will be the winners?

Some people have in the past experienced inner conflict as they traded. Maybe the methods or style they had adopted did not fit their personality, or were at odds with other people's values. The family person who chose a method which involved trading 'round the clock' or which led to them missing the important dates in the kids' diaries, may have felt themselves to be at odds with themselves inside.

This was the sort of situation which could have led to poor judgement and bad decisions. When they made the right decision for the kids, to close their book and go to the concert, was it the wrong time in the market. Did it miss an opportunity?

Look at your whole life style, values and attitudes. Look around you at your environment and your stakeholders, and all the other factors that are really important to you. Now ask yourself if there is anything inside suggesting you can make some changes for the better? You will want to be at your best at all times, because then you are increasing your chances of success and feeling good about it.

What do you want to change? Ensure there are no conflicts within. Combine your problem solving skills with inner and outer awareness, an understanding of your whole environment. Build more stability into your life. Be constructively aware of the consequences of every decision you make and own them.

Some people may have asked 'is it worth it' - the commitment and willingness to be continually involved and focused. Others may have felt pain, emotion, stress or distress when things did not work out. Limiting beliefs may have got in the way until they were removed - an irrational fear of failure or losing money as opposed to the ability to calmly and rationally recognise and learn from mistakes and errors of judgement.

Nobody likes to be around a loser, except possibly another loser. Did you ever see yourself as a loser, or are you an achiever riding the normal cycles in the market, confident in your own ability and judgement for the duration?

Mechanical systems can of course take any emotion and feeling out of trading. This may be a good thing, but you must still choose which system to follow, or who to give your money to, to manage. And wouldn't you rather enjoy the thrill of winning with your own intellectual, emotional and financial resources, progressively learning and positively growing from the occasional setback. Manage your emotions to enjoy your life. Seek the positive. Use your left brain to trade the system and your right brain to enjoy and share your success.

We have talked of internal dialogue and there is external dialogue also. Associate yourself with the right crowd, having a similar perspective and optimism about life. Enjoy the shared moments of reflection, away from the market. Escape to a haven of peace, to enjoy good food, good coffee, or just good company. Talk about families, values, leisure, sports. Recharge the batteries. Use only positive language. Gee the other guy up, objectively. Be generous of spirit and receive the dividends modestly.

Meanwhile, the Internet is improving the mechanics and knowledge of trading daily. You can do all you do from home. You may be on your own, but you were never lonely. You may miss the market buzz and the exchange of ideas and you can be wholly objective. You will have more time with your stakeholders and you can always choose to get out and play golf, tennis...

You choose your environment and your lifestyle. Day trading gives you the best of both options. As trading offices and cybercafes grow in your neighbourhood, you can work nearer to home, having the best of both worlds.

Remember, crowd psychology often reflects the lowest common denominator. The 'herd instinct' does not necessarily exhibit highly intelligent behaviour. You can be above all this, with the opportunity for your chosen life-style, both during trading and facilitated by the success of trading.

The Power to Influence Others

Any market is a mass of people. Have you ever been at a sports event and felt the power and excitement of the crowd. As I was writing this book, 101 million shares in Marks & Spencer changed hands in one day. This is the company which above all has represented small shareholders' hopes and dreams in the UK since the war. The stories abound of how you could buy 1,000 share after the War and be a millionaire now. When take-over rumours started in the market, thousands of small investors wanted to be on board.

Have you ever seen a queue, or a crowd gathered around something and not been intrigued to know what the big deal was. When you're trading on your own and you see a sharp movement in a share, what are the thoughts that go through you?

We are all individuals, unique in our makeup, values, attitudes and beliefs. Other people may have similar motives and goals from their trading, and everyone is different. This book has never represented itself as a technical textbook on trading, it is more about the psychology of the individual.

Markets are a collection of individual psychologies, and they often represent crowd behaviours. When the market rises 300 points in a day, it could be driven by a small number of trades by big investors, together with marking up by dealers. Or it could be driven by a lot of trades.

When a day trader is sat at their own computer, dealing on the Internet, or at a screen in a day-trading office, where are they getting their information from? Their judgement on where the market is going may be driven by what they see on the screen, what they hear from others, in person or by phone, or what they feel inside, or a combination of these. What is it for you? How do you form your view or get a feel for where the market or the stock you are watching is going today?

We talked earlier about representation systems and strategies. Now you have understood your own motivation and decision strategies, and how you process internally, in how many ways can that add to the quality of your trading? Here's another factor: how to influence people, including yourself.

Very few individuals can influence the crowd. It would take a great deal of money to influence one company's shares, let alone the market. Some people may have felt it was impossible to stand against the crowd. How long could you stand fishing in the middle of a torrent? How about fishing in another stream, or in a quieter part of the river, where the fish lie deep? By all means make money out of going with the crowd. And how much more satisfaction do you get when you have researched a situation yourself, watched carefully for the moment to move and made a turn before the crowd spotted the situation?

When I bought the shares at 192, I had been following them for some time. What better time to buy them than the day when I felt the market to be oversold? I bought as many as the dealers would sell to me at the quoted price. There were no other buyers. Crowd markets are often driven sharply in one direction by relatively little business. The market makers see or anticipate a situation and mark the prices accordingly. When the buyers returned to the shares I bought, they were marked up quickly. I bought more at 220 and 230 and within a week they were 300.

In trading, you can be prepared to be alone even when you're with others. Make your own decisions when trading and by all means enjoy yourself outside the trading. When I took exams as a youngster, there was always someone doing a 'post-mortem' afterwards. Eventually I noticed that they appeared either to be 'crowing' at those who had missed the points they had got, or they were bemoaning what they had missed themselves. In the main, it seemed that people became more worried than they needed to be after the post-mortem. Then they had weeks to wait for the outcome.

Did you ever make your mind up about a bet you were going to make, maybe on a horse, and before you got to the pay desk you spoke to someone who belittled your choice and had a 'sure thing'? Did you ever change your mind, after all the research you had done and ended up with a loser? Did you ever bet on the favourite simply because it was the favourite? If everyone bet on the favourite, who apart from the bookmakers would make money.

Prices in the markets are largely determined by supply and demand. For every buyer there is a seller. In how many ways can you improve your percentage success. If you trade with the average, will you even get average performance when your dealing and fixed costs are taken into account? One thing you can be sure of: whatever you think you are, you are much more than that.

Successful people appear to have the power to influence others, consciously or unconsciously. We all have that power. We can all model our behaviours on excellent behaviours we see elsewhere. If at this stage anyone had a limiting belief pop into their mind, they already know how to have removed that by now.

Rapport is one of the 'buzzwords' of the 21st century. How do you create rapport easily and effortlessly with anyone you choose? How do you do it with yourself? Think back to that time when you felt so much in tune with someone else and consciously or unconsciously you could see how well you were getting on together. Did it feel as if you were in a bubble together, or as if time stood still, the rest of the world melted away… Did you have a feeling, maybe from your centre that you knew you were in what you now understand to be rapport?

How did you do that? Not by consciously thinking and planning. It came from inside, effortlessly and easily. As you go back to that time now, notice how good it felt and how easily you did it without trying. What do you see, hear and feel as you're in that time right now…

And was there ever a time when you felt you could do anything, even for a brief moment, a time when it felt so good… Then you were in rapport with yourself.

All of us have the talents to create rapport, to be powerfully persuasive with others and ourselves, to be in flow, or in the zone.

In the 30-day programme, you will learn how to create rapport with anyone, including yourself. You will also learn how to learn. You will understand the language of eye accessing cues, mirroring and matching and the way to transform a situation you are in through perceptual positions and sensory acuity.

Research shows that we make a lasting impression on a stranger in the first four seconds of our meeting. four seconds! It used to be 14 seconds. I have worked in Executive recruitment and I understood that, after the first five minutes, even the very best candidate would not change the interviewer's impression of them.

Now, you and I can choose to be different and understand much more about each other. And yet, how much of ourselves are we wearing 'outside ourselves' in our neurophysiology? In NLP Practitioner or Master Practitioner training, we have been trained above all to respect another person's model of the world. One of the earliest skills we learned was to calibrate someone's whole neurophysiology.

If we were conversing now, you would be deriving only about 7% of your own interpretation and understanding from the words themselves. Then 38% would come from the way I said the words (intonation, etc.) and 55% from non-verbal communication (similar to what Desmond Morris called body language).

So, what is it like for others to be trading? We may never know, because we are not them, we did not have their upbringing, their genes, their environment. We may believe we have similar values, attitudes and beliefs and maybe that's how we seem to relate to them or like to be around them. We are all as unique as a snowflake and infinitely more complex. The cells that are in you did not just appear from nowhere. They were once in other living beings, plants, water, rock, the atmosphere, etc. We are all part of a connected universe and every one of us is different.

When we believe we understand someone else, we can only understand our own filtered version of someone else. Perception is projection and everything we recognise in someone else is a projection of something inside ourself. Otherwise, how would we know how it looked, sounded or felt?

So realise that we are all different and all unique. Take account of that and use it to your limitless benefit in your trading.

I'm not talking about taking the maverick view for the sake of it. We are understanding the importance of choice and owning the consequence.

Stephen Covey wrote about the Seven Habits of Highly Effective People. We are all highly effective at all we do, otherwise we wouldn't be able to do it. Someone tells me they are a failure. How long does it take to become an alcoholic? How hard did a person have to practice before they became world class at drinking? How often do they have to do it every day to 'keep their hand in'? So how long did it take for that other person to become a failure? And did you ever think that anything less than total failure is success at not failing?

By all means understand the habits and patterns of others who you regard as being highly successful. Then ask yourself how you know they are highly successful? Are you just convinced by the words of someone else, or what you see or do you have a feeling? Whichever way works for you, how do you know they are successful unless you know…and you do you know, you know… So when are you going to be as successful at trading as you are at breathing, or eating, or watching TV, or knowing that someone else is highly successful…

So watch and understand others' moves. Model the best and beat the rest. And you might add to that baseline tennis.

When Bjorn Borg won Wimbledon six times, he did it basically by standing on the baseline and knocking the ball back into the other guy's court. He waited, patiently for the opportunity to strike, for the other guy to make a mistake. Andre Agassi does a lot of the same thing, only he hits the ball harder and harder. No-one works harder round the court than Agassi. He has the shots, OK, and he also has the confidence, the self-belief, an eye for the narrow window of opportunity that wins point after point after point

When you're with people and you are creating superb rapport, how do we communicate? How can you get people to tell you what you want to hear. First, you ask open questions (the ones that need more than a yes or no). Then, you listen, with your ears and all your senses, you pick up all the cues they are giving you. Did you ever see anyone who said yes, while their head shook from side to side. This was incongruent. Their neurophysiology was giving the real answer.

So in how many ways are you already seeing the possibilities for using these skills that you really knew you always had? And when you have unpacked them and polished and adjusted them and maybe practised even more than you were already doing, and repacked them, what are the opportunities you can see or feel you have for yourself, what are you telling yourself you can do now, in your trading and your life?

Different markets have different characters. One of them is you. The only market that matters is the one that takes place in you. You have the goals and aspirations, you have the plan, the strategy, the methodology and the style. You decide what to do and when, knowing you and you alone are responsible for the consequences. You assess the performance against the benchmarks you set or accepted for yourself. You review, you learn, you improve, you grow, you succeed, by someone's benchmark, somewhere in the world, at all that you do.

Like the markets, you never stop - 24 hours a day, seven days a week, there is something going on somewhere. While you sleep, your unconscious mind analyses, compares, reviews, reassesses, reorganises, stores, etc. Intuition and inspiration come from the unconscious. The facts are there, listen for the ideas.

And when you're in the thick of things, immersed in the sights and sounds of the market, you can still find space for yourself, through the peripheral vision exercise, through meditation, and by going somewhere else, an environment which is very different, where your thoughts can happen naturally, where the helpful little voice can come up with its suggestions. Wherever you go, you are always there, consciously and unconsciously and, now that you can create rapport with anyone, especially yourself, you can be an individual as part of the crowd that makes the market exciting.

Chapter 6

How are you doing? - confidence, motivation and resilience

Now that you can look from outside yourself and see your self as you really are, inside, where do you know you keep your confidence and self-belief? You already know from anchors that you can go back to a time when you felt good about yourself, even for a moment and how does that feel right now? When you are in the thick of trading, listening and noticing all that there is to understand and you can match that against all that you already know, you can reach back to that moment of self-belief which is always there.

Trading may have once been coloured by emotions and stress, limiting beliefs, fear of failure, of losing money. Learning from mistakes and misjudgements wasn't the only skill you have acquired during the reading of this book which by reading it thus far means that you have chosen to leave any old unresourceful patterns behind you. As the sun shines today and everyday, outside you or inside you, that means that you can see, hear and feel even more clearly the talents and qualities that were shaded or hidden until now.

And what of the new levels of confidence, motivation and resilience that are creeping into your thoughts even as you read this word and the next few thousand that come between now and the end of this book? In how many different ways will they pervade your professional, measured, strategic, successful trading? As you go forward in time to a time when you knew you had experienced the benefits of all these changes even then having noticed the signs of success, how good is that feeling inside you know?

Mechanical trading is for some who prefer others like you to make your own decisions and be programmed for success. You can choose either to settle for automated trading, or some mechanical system means you have the confidence either way.

Some people have dwelt in the past. Regret was an emotion from the past and fear was a feeling about a different future. For the present, I give you these thoughts, because all that matters to you is the present.

There is no right or wrong in the market, besides what is right for you. You set the rules, you make the plays, you assess the situation, you have the benchmarks ready for your success. There are no good trades or bad trades. Everything is right in its own context and everything is as it should be. If you lost $10,000 dollars on a trade and then the market went up, the only difference was time. If you had been on holiday that day, the loss didn't materialise. If the market went down after you closed the trade, you ended up with a smile on your face, as you bought back cheaper.

If anything ever didn't work out for you in the past, the time or the context were misplaced. Life is about choices and timing and if things didn't work out quite as hoped, you made the best of it, maybe reframed the context and moved forward yet again. If you had negative patterns and programs and you had found yourself wanting to hang onto them, what was the purpose for yourself? And why would you have wanted to trade until you have now changed all that.

Trading is evolution and personal growth. It is what it is, because it has every aspect that is in life. Now that you can trade whenever you feel it is right, that means you have the courage to continue to see your way through any ups and downs and achieve the goals you have set yourself. The motivation is your own, towards those aims and everything else that they imply.

Some people may have experienced pain in trading. If this had happened repeatedly, what message was there? Pain and disappointment are states we may have produced in ourselves, which until they had been eliminated were masking the possibilities and opportunities. If you knew someone who had lost regularly, how much skill did that take and what was the innermost goal it was meeting? If someone could beat the odds on the downside, consistently, they have an extraordinary set of unconscious skills to read the market.

You can see it differently, and there is no failure, only feedback, learning, growth and experience. How did you cope with apparent setbacks until you could see the whole picture. How much money could you make if the curve was always flat and there was no volatility. Who would want to continually lose commissions, costs, spread and margin because there were no ups and downs? You trade because there are ups and downs. So, how do you fit your method and mentality to the saw tooth opportunities before you?

Try this...Go inside and find your mood now. Score it on a scale from minus 100 to plus 100. OK. Now, go back briefly to a time which was the worst. And as you are in that time now, where would you score that, between minus 100 and plus 100? And finally, go back to a time which was the very best and be in that time now, seeing what you saw, hearing what you heard and feeling what you felt. Where would you score that?

So now come back to now and think of the seat you are sitting in. When you read the word now, go to that old worst time...and to that very best time, now...and finally to that time a few moments ago, where you first started to score...and how did you do that? How did you move your internal state down, up and back to where you were, so elegantly and rapidly that you know you can control your state as you want to. Didn't you...

Risk and Reward

So we were conditioned in so many patterns: win or lose; success and failure; risk and reward. You can earn a reward in trading without understanding and accepting risk, and how much better can you do when you understand now that you define risk and reward. If it is defined outside you, either it does not fit for you, or you have chosen to take on someone else's model of the world, or that old belief that you don't need any more. Trading for you, is how you can make risk work for you.

You determine: the types of risk; how much risk; an assessment of the risk; and whether you choose to trade with the appraisal of the potential consequences. You decide the goals and you determine the measures of success. You determine the circumstances in which you will change your stance, add more risk or reduce it. You alone get the rewards for all your decisions and they go well beyond money.

You don't need to be a mathematician to instinctively understand probability and make it work for you. The market is a nil sum game and there is more than enough stupidity and unprofessionalism elsewhere for you to make a good living from it...or even better. Good and bad trades were a product of someone else's mind in the now, not the past. You, meanwhile, see only effective and ineffective trades in the context of your goals and your strategy. When they were in the past you made an inefficient decision, based on inaccurate or incomplete analysis, or emotion. Even a good trade could make a loss, the question is did it beat the market?

Success and Failure

Success and failure are attitudes or beliefs. They are based on patterns we learned in childhood. We are programmed to achieve. Otherwise, how do we stay alive? Do we have to ask all the organs and cells in our bodies to perform exactly as well as they do, or does the blueprint of perfect health in our higher self maintain everything in the good condition it is. Where you knew someone who became ill, how did they do that? Do you know what a miracle it is to be able to sustain a cold or flu for days on end, when you are programmed for cells in your body to strive for perfect health.

Now that we realise all the skills we have that do so much for us in every aspect of our daily lives, which run in our unconscious mind, how much more can we do? So, whether small or large, think of all the things you ever succeeded at in your life. Start with 'I succeeded in getting dressed on my own today'. Just try in vain to stop all those successful thoughts which are popping into your mind. No ifs, buts, explanations or justifications, just simple, raw, achievement and success. Now, as they keep on coming, try not to stop laughing inside yourself or outside yourself.

So what is it in success that we may have overlooked if we ever scored ourselves at less than that? What is present in success that is not present at other times? What is not present in success that is present at other times? What is not present in those other times that is not present in success as well? What is not present in success that is not present in success at other times either? Finally, realising that failure was never a choice that you wanted to make, in how many different ways can you represent success in your mind? What does it look, sound, feel, smell or taste like? Fill your senses with success now.

Later we shall deal with anchors and reframes. Whenever you have a powerful, positive feeling (and just for a moment try in vain to stop even one of those successful memories you just had from seeping back into your consciousness), anchor it. Decide the different categories of good and powerful feelings you can recall and anchor them wherever you feel they are most accessible when you want them.

Failure in one person's model of the world can be success in someone else's. Fran thought she had failed when she lost money trading. Bill thought Fran must be incredibly successful to have the money to trade. James was in awe that Fran was successfully courageous in trading. Bob thought they were all incredibly successful to just get out of bed in the mornings. So ask yourself now, "will it be by the end of today or lunchtime tomorrow when I have realised in how many ways I can already be successful and the many opportunities there are to learn and grow"?

There have even been people who were frightened of success. This might have been just as limiting as fear of failure. Those other people may have grabbed a profit as soon as they saw it, or run their losses. I was like that once. Not any more. Others might have lacked self-confidence and been easily persuaded or influenced away from a chosen path by friends or analysts, or even the newspapers, or a sudden temporary change of price. I was like that. Not any more.

Two things I learned in the past. Analysts and economists are better at explaining the past than predicting the future. People seemed very eloquent at recounting the one that got away, the terrible bad luck, the trades they should have done. They produced faultless logic to explain and justify. How successful are they when they use those same elegant skills to analyse, prepare, observe, trade, observe, reverse the trade, bank the gains. How good can we be explaining inside how clever we are at all the things we choose to do, as we run our own lives and trading is our whole responsibility.

Henry was a perfectionist. I asked him why? He said he was frightened of failure. I pointed out that anything less than total and utter failure in everything he did was not perfection. When he opened his mouth, the words would not come out, but he breathed as he gasped. Life goes on...

Fear and Motivation, Loss and Stress

I thought long and hard before putting anything with negative connotations in this book. Who could possibly be upset by all this positive thinking? Fear and motivation have been linked for some. We talked elsewhere of the Meta programs. When someone had a filter of being driven 'away from' failure, they might well have achieved. And how much more can they achieve now that they are driven towards success.

Negative motivation towards a goal was driven by patterns from the past. Once we have removed those old emotions, all the while keeping the learnings, we can have positive motivation.

It is said we live in a world of stress. I guess this is something I feel from time to time. Adrenaline can be a mixed blessing. It is, after all, the most powerful drug we know. If you choose to have stress, understand it and control it. Make it work for you. You may have noticed a stress 'curve' (like the chart of a share price) as you experienced the market's highs and lows, pre, during or post a trade.

So let's do this for a moment. Imagine you have bought some stock and the price is going down steadily. How do you feel inside? Now imagine that you've just bought and the price is going up steadily. Now how do you feel?

Now imagine you just sold that stock and the price is going on up, even faster than before. How do you feel now? Or you just sold the stock and the price is going through the floor. How does that feel?

How did you do that? How did you manage to feel bad when the price was going down and going up! Context my friend. You can run all these feelings without even thinking about them. You can produce exactly the state you want, with the right trigger. So change the script. Remember a time when you were feeling really great about a trade, while it was in play. And see what you saw, hear what you heard and feel what you felt, inside yourself as you relive that moment right now. And make the picture as powerful as possible. Anchor it.

So now that you know how great that can feel, think of a time when you felt awful about a trade that was in play. As you are in that moment, grab the feelings of that positive memory from your anchor and now see, hear and feel what happened to that old negative memory.

Is paper trading the same as reality? No, I hear you say. If you were playing the neighbours at Monopoly, did you ever get really fired up about it? But its only a game, and on paper at that. You can play out all your strategies, methods and moves on paper, to get the feel of how well they can work. Do you think they let trainee dealers start completely raw with other peoples' money? Do they let airline pilots fly, with no time on the simulator?

You can dry run everything you plan to do, a system or whatever. When you realise how well you can do it, then you are motivated. Ah, I heard someone say that it's not like the real thing.

So go to your favourite beach right now and imagine you can see the sun set over the sea. It's warm, as you know it and you can see all the sights, hear all the sounds and feel all you feel right now. Oh no, don't close your eyes and do it. What is that feeling of calmness that comes over you?

Intensify any imagined experience and it can seem so real. Fear is an emotion of the future. If you had been confronted by a wild animal, the pattern might have been learned in the past, but the fear was what would happen next, or even the possibility of the worst.

So, if you had ever had any vivid experience of fear, how can you use those same skills of imagination to experience the thrill, pleasure, joy, warmth, etc of success.

You can make a feeling so real you can almost smell it. So go out to trade.

Stress is a state created in ourselves. Resilience is a quality we have to have come so far. We are all mortal. This is the only certainty in life. While we are here this once, what are we going to do with life?

When you have traded and felt pressure or stress, it was a function of your position, size and an internal state that only you can create for yourself. Why on earth would you want to do that? If you were world class at failing, you could do the throbbing temples, the hammering heart, the perspiring brow, the racing thoughts, the vivid images of disastrous outcomes, the sounds of other peoples' voices berating you and that deep feeling in your guts, at will. And if you imagined even one of those states as you read that, will it be tomorrow or next Monday when you have decided to start being totally wildly successful?

Luck, repeating mistakes, conflict, anguish, frustration are all states people have created inside themselves. One day, I had a terrible headache. I had no idea where it came from. Pills wouldn't touch it. I decided I was not going to do this.

I found a quiet spot, settled down, closed my eyes and went back to the last time I knew I had felt incredibly well. I filled myself with those well feelings and in my mind I created a glass ball. I poured the feelings into the glass ball and, in my mind, carefully transported the ball back to the now. Finally, when I knew I was in the now, carefully holding the glass ball, I poured those wonderful well feelings, in my mind's eye, down through the top of my head and through to all parts of me. Within an hour the headache had left me, never to return.

All the skills and all the feelings and all the successes you plan to have, or ever had, are in your mind now and forever. So, flood your senses with them and start to be the successful trader you always dreamt you can be now that you are trading.

If you ever had a fear of money, remove it now, or stop trading. God made the world, God made us in his own image. God made money. Make money your friend. Grow to love money and remember to give some back. To achieve all your potential help to keep the universe in balance. Give something of yourself to the universe every day and watch the universe provide.

Money is an illusion we created to facilitate trade. It grows in value without you doing anything, through the mechanism of inflation. Any number of people waste it, so be your very, very best and get the money flowing in. Use it for yourself and your stakeholders and remember those who have not yet recognised all that you already know about yourself.

Self-Confidence and Self-Esteem

Be careful. Whatever you do, don't let that self-confidence and self-esteem build inside you. Promise me that you will keep on constant alert for that spark of confidence or that warm feeling, the positive voice inside you, which can catch you unawares if you are not vigilant. You must watch for it night and day, because I warn you. Self-confidence and self-esteem are addictive. Once you have tried a bit, it will grow inside you like a thundercloud, building and spreading up and across the sky. Once you let it get hold of you, there will be no stopping it.

People talk about positive mental attitude. That is one of the fundamentals of NLP. Only, we are talking about more than PMA. There are many courses and books which tell of or teach PMA. If you adopt, repeat and reinforce a positive mental attitude to anything and everything in your life, you may already have found many of the ways you have changed for the better.

Using the techniques in this book, you can go several steps further. First, you may already have eliminated negative beliefs, patterns and programs which may in the past have held you back. You may have elicited and changed your values, to substantially positive. You may be using anchors and reframes to bring so much more positivity into your life and especially your trading. You may be meditating regularly, eating a balanced diet and drinking more water.

When you go inside, you may already find signs that all these many positive steps you have taken are growing day by day. We can institute a positive attitude and a positive set of beliefs and how much better is it being pervaded by positivity, having found the way to release old negative emotions which may have been holding you back, so that you can move forward in a positive frame of mind at will. Please try in vain, now, to not have all those positive feelings which are growing in you now.

Look out for negative thinkers and don't wish that they could be as positive as you. By all means give them a fair hearing. Listen to their woeful tales and warnings and compare your own positive feelings. Smile down deep inside you from your head to your toes, letting the warmth of your good feelings about yourself pervade every cell in your self.

When you have seen negative feelings in the past, you may have asked yourself "where did that come from" and, having gone inside, you could have cleaned up with that internal cleansing spray that we all can find, leaving the sparkling glint of positivity shining from within.

Now you are moving forward in every aspect of your trading, you may have learned the most effective techniques, you may be practising with real professionalism each and every day. You may have access to the best technology and the most sophisticated systems. Even the most expensive equipment you buy could not guarantee success until you had mastered yourself and your own choices. Remember, there are no systems and no technology in the world that can be as sophisticated as those that you already possess inside you.

How many muscles are there in your body? How many nerve cells throughout your body-mind? You are receiving up to two million bits of information at any one moment. Without your conscious thought, your unconscious is filtering, sorting, analysing, comparing, processing, deleting, etc. all this information. Some people have become overwhelmed by the amount of information bombarding their conscious senses daily. And yet, your unconscious mind is processing more information in a day than the entire air traffic controller systems of the world, often as you relax!.

How much can you do now that you realise the power of the partnership between your conscious and unconscious mind? Trusting your unconscious, are you going to wait till tomorrow to see the limitless positive effects this awesome power is having on every aspect of all these things you have limitless potential to do now?

By all means practise, review, learn from the past and improve, for there is no substitute for consistency of self-belief and being in flow. And, having put in train those practical, conscious initiatives, ask yourself who is driving your bus? The plain truth is, you are. The whole of you that you have begun to glimpse. For what highest positive purpose for yourself would you have wanted in any way to restrict this limitless potential by the relatively much slower processes of your conscious mind?

Self-confidence and self-belief are just that. Belief and confidence in your self. Think of the one person in the world in whom you have the greatest confidence. No more than 55% of you is appraising this person unconsciously. You are aware of yourself unconsciously, 100% of the time. Since you were born, life's experiences had put in your way the residue of some of the negative experiences you had had. Once you were whole and had none of that.

Think of a fence that faces a horse, galloping in the country. It was planted or erected by someone. The horse rarely refuses: it sails over it, or crashes through it and the might of its power continues across the landscape ahead. If you are the rider, preparing the course, in how many ways can you think of removing or avoiding the fence as any possible obstacle to your progress. This was a fence built by man or woman and in an instant in you mind it doesn't exist any more. And once it was open fields where you can ride and ride...

There never has been any bar or obstacle to your success in trading other than your unconscious erected at some time in the past. The builder of the arch knows exactly how to place the keystone such that it holds the entire structure. The maker of the chain instinctively knows the weakest link. The architect of the building knows the exact spot to place the charges so that the structure can fall safely in one go exactly where it was planned. Your unconscious mind knows all of these things and...knowing...

Chapter 7

How can you improve? - the Continuous Cycle of Success

Markets have been around for a long time. The biggest developments in recent years include: derivatives; trading on the Internet; and the huge growth in the volume of speculative currency trading. Many of the traditional trading methods, strategies and styles are well established. You may have had your own well-oiled approach for some time. One would always wish to be prepared for new factors in the market, however. This is part of the regular review you will carry out and your peripheral openness and awareness of change.

Review of these developments and the success of your own methods is part of the professional approach you are now bringing to your trading. There are quiet times in the market, when it is wise to stay on the sidelines. Without volatility, trading opportunities are reduced. However, this is also a time for review and rationalisation of your portfolio. What if any are the new factors and how has the market performed or behaved since you last reviewed?

Review, like trading, is a time to balance logic and intuition. What does your analysis tell you: about yourself; about your opportunities to learn and grow; about the trends and possible consequences? What does your instinct or 'feel' tell you?

Most of all, how can you improve and grow the new, positive patterns of success in your own behaviours and their implementation in the domain of the markets?

Creativity and Innovation

Many people may have feared change. To the onlooker, the market may seem like ordered chaos. Change and apparent chaos can bring huge opportunity for you, now that you are seeing things differently. If it is true that change threatens other people, that already gives you an edge. Your new skills make change work for you. As for chaos, the world is in chaos.

Of course, if the present state is exactly determinable, then the future is predictable. Markets are the product of innumerable organisations, their employees and customers; they are regulated or overlooked by other institutions; they are taxed by government and in the public eye; most are subject to changing environmental conditions, directly or indirectly. They are in chaos.

When you can find any order here, you have an advantage over anyone else who sees simply chaos. You can bring your own order to the game by having your own systems, which you know will work for you, because in results terms, only you matter. You determine the measures of success; you enjoy that success; you reinvest that success; you review and improve that success.

You must be able to think independently and creatively, if necessary in a contrary way, but not just for the sake of it. You are just as creative as the next person, in your own terms. You are an independent spirit and being, having an impact on your immediate environment, and able to choose and control the way you perceive and manage that environment. In this book, you have all the tools and skills to augment your existing talents and capabilities; to review, remove or change your beliefs; to change your values to wholly positive; to set your own mission and goals and, in visualising the successful outcome, to create and program your own future.

In life, change is the only constant. In your positive frame of mind, change brings increasing options. We discussed at the start of this book, the levels of change - the levels at which you perceive change and at which it happens, for you.

One of my skills is lateral thinking. I don't know how I got it, or how I do it, without thinking. I can tell you how to create lateral thought for yourself, however. In markets, where behaviours may often be driven down tramlines and the herd instinct may exist, your ability to think laterally will make creative difference in your success.

Chunking

Think, for a moment, of your favourite food. What is this an example of? You might say nourishment. What is nourishment an example of? You might say health. What is health an example of?...You can keep on chunking up towards more and more abstract levels.

Now go back to that food. What is a component of that food? You may say tomato sauce. What is a component of tomato sauce? Water. What is a component of water? Oxygen. What is a component of oxygen? An atom...etc. This is chunking down.

Sometimes, in the market, you may need inspiration. Find it in yourself, by using your natural skills to create a lateral thought. The process is, to take the existing subject, chunk up, move to a parallel channel and chunk down.

In the film 'Working Girl' Emily Griffith sees a market where the focus is on TV and telecommunications.

She has a hunch about radio. She sells it to the client and it wins. To achieve that thought, she could have looked at TV. Then she could ask what TV was an example of? (Chunk up). Communications. What is another example of communications? (Chunk down). Radio. That is how you create lateral thought. That is also how you may be able to resolve negotiations or disagreement.

Submodalities

We all create internal representations. Each of us has their own process. Every internal representation is made up of aspects or components which Bandler and Grinder called submodalities.

For example, as you think of a vivid memory of when you felt you could do anything, was the picture colour or black and white? Was it moving or still? You can go through the entire list of 'submodalities', including the components of any sounds or feelings that may have been there.

Now, take a situation where you need to be resourceful, or where you may have been unresourceful in the past. Elicit and compare the submodalities of each. Determine the key difference or differences. Now take the component which has the strongest impact on the representation of your good or successful experiences and make a parallel change in your unresourceful situation. What now appears different to you. Now do you have the insight you need?

Changes in practical style can dramatically affect trading performance, especially if they are the result of careful analysis and review. Now add the change in your own personal perceptions and style for your self and see what happens. Continue to observe, review and adjust until the new style is comfortable for you. Before putting it into practice, you can also visualise your successful outcome, 'dry run' the movie of the upcoming situation (a 'dress-rehearsal') and then watch how you succeed and how did that feel?

The law of probabilities suggests that both successful systems and the herd instinct will converge to the average. With creativity and review this need not be the case. Toss a coin 100 times and the odds will always be 50:50 that it will come down heads. Beat the market 50 times and you still have your original probability for which way the price will go next (unless the company goes bust).

You are improving yourself, your perception and performance, through review and creativity. You are looking to beat your own averages, not the market. For you, you are the market. Of course, millions of other people have an effect on which way the market goes, and your review means that you can continually move at the right time to the best prospect.

Fund managers' performance is measured against the index. As the size and spread of their portfolio grows, their chances of beating the average decline. As computer generated trades proliferate, they may at times set the market trend, but they will converge on the average. You can determine your own average and beat it day after day.

Modelling

It has been said that trading and successful investment requires a special set of talents that few possess. Once upon a time, this was the conventional belief about skiing. Now anyone can learn to ski.

Ski boards were only invented recently. These new techniques had to be specially evolved, through balance and synchronised movement. How quickly did you learn to walk? Were you instructed, bit by bit, exactly how to configure and move all the hundreds of individual muscles you use? Or did you observe and model other humans around you?

NLP has shown us how, through modelling we have already observed and acquired the skills and strategies we have understood. If you wish, you can consciously unpack, understand and apply the skills and strategies you see in others. Better still, to 'stand in their shoes'.

I watched Nick Faldo, over and over, not to learn his golf techniques and mechanical movements, but to get a sense or a feeling of what it was like to be him as he played a great golf shot. This is insight and intuition. If I could have met him personally, I might have asked him to go minutely through his motivation, decision, convincer and reassurance strategies for hitting the great shot. All the while, I could watch his eye movements and listen to his predicates, to get an understanding of everything that was happening for him inside and out. I could then exactly model these.

Modelling is a skill we all have. Most things we learned as young children were unconsciously modelled from those around us. Our skills and our strategies. Being required to watch and listen, when adults were around, we not only learned the skills we saw, but also learned how adults unconsciously modelled other adults and the results they got. We took inside what worked and didn't work.

Trading is an unstructured environment. You can put your own structure on it and one which is right and works for you and you alone. You can now take any aspect of trading: the strategy; style; methodology; mentality; etc. and add to that the models you have seen to be highly successful around you. Some may be conscious. Many followed Jim Slater's 'Zulu' principle, with great success. Others may have sought to emulate Warren Buffett's successful strategies and methodologies. How much better now that you can listen to, watch and get a feel for, model and apply, Mr Buffett's internal strategies.

Anchors and reframes

With all that you have seen, felt, internally processed and understood, from this short text, you now have more than enough to run one winning strategy after another.

As a beginner, you have a head start over experienced traders, as you can watch and learn from their mistakes, model their best strategies - practical or psychological, test drive your own systems, processes and methodologies and start out as a winner in your own perception.

As an experienced trader, many of these words have already struck a chord, felt right or looked good to augment or dramatically improve your past performance. In addition, you now have the understanding to set and measure everything on your own terms, not someone else's. If they happen to coincide with someone else, that's OK and be sure they are still your own. You are driving the bus. Success and failure are now concepts defined only by you - for you.

To enhance your performance and your positive states even more, you can change for the better every situation you find yourself in. By enhancing the positives of your state while you prepare, before you trade, while you trade and when you review, to improve, you can now create limitless positive frames of mind. The processes you will use are anchors and reframes.

Anchors

In the appendix are practical exercises for you to do to improve skills which you already have.

Did you ever hear someone say "they're playing our tune"? The tune was an anchor. The unconscious mind latched onto a happy experience the music that was playing at the time, or which afterwards seemed appropriate. I cannot listen to Enigma without melting into the first few moments in which I met my life partner, Heather. The music is anchored to the memory.

And so it is with you, in a myriad of ways. And how will it be now you have perceived the possibilities to use anchors in your current trading...or your life? Before you leave home, or go to your PC or phone to start trading, you can anchor yourself into a positive frame of mind.

As you review the markets, yesterday's performance, your portfolio and any other pertinent information before commencing your moves for the day, you can fire an anchor which you previously set, returning your neurophysiology to the time when you made the best decisions.

Before beginning trading, you can fire your anchor of calmness and observed detachment. When a decision point approaches, you fire your optimal decision making anchor.

As you review your decisions, you are in a state recalled by an anchor of calm reflection and outstanding judgement.

When you win, you stack the euphoria of success to your existing success anchor. If things don't work out, you fire another appropriate anchor which moves you into the frame for learning and growing. And on...

Reframes

Add to these the ability to reframe any context, behaviour or event.

One of your investments or trades underperforms your expectations, or registers a loss. Look around you at those who have lost more; at the market index which fell much further than your investment. As the market continues to fall, notice the growing benefits of being out of the loss-making situation and how much more attractive your stock is growing with each point it falls.

On a day which didn't work out quite as expected, go home to the people you love and watch their miraculous movements, enjoy the miracle of life. Reflect on your excellent judgement in selecting a partner with those good qualities. Or, as you walk to the car, notice the dropouts, homeless, less fortunate than you. Give something back from your pocket, even your last dime, to help rebalance the universe towards you.

You can think of any number of situations you can reframe from positive to negative, realising as you do, how you can grow and become what you always dreamed you are.

Epilogue

This book never pretended that it was a textbook on trading and investment. You, dear reader, already have the skills to trade successfully and the ability to learn and grow from all that you see, hear and feel around you.

Your unconscious mind will already have realised much of this reproduced in this book. Having opened your eyes and your mind, as you read and understood, each day your unconscious is making new connections. Don't dare to sleep, lest you might find you have woken up with yet another step change in your ability. If you so much as blink, you may have missed a moment in the continuum of your achievement. Try in vain to ignore all the signs that have been there for some time, that your success at trading has grown.

We have shared an introduction to some of the elements of NLP which, as Bandler and Grinder set out to find, represent the language and behaviours we are implementing consciously and unconsciously, day and night, all our lives. Model the best and... you know the rest.

Don't follow the 30-day program unless you want to be successful beyond what you ever dreamed you can be. One technique alone, having mastered it, will have a subtle or obvious impact on your trading success.

Why did you read this far, other than to be your very best? You can learn and grow with each day, in ways which go far beyond your trading. The only question is...will you start today, or wait until tomorrow?

Thank you

30 Day Programme of Achievement

What this program is about - creating a positive, powerful self for trading

I am taking it for granted that before you embark on this program, you at least know what trading is about and probably have already traded. You should have a clear idea of the trading techniques you will use, the resources and information you will draw on and a pretty clear strategy for your trades. You will also be totally committed to approach trading in a professional frame of mind. Anything less than this and you may be gambling. That is your choice.

In order to realise your limitless potential and be your very best, your body and your mind need to be in good condition. Many of the exercises in this program will help you achieve the latter.

Day 1 - Caring for yourself

The 'mind-body' connection is now proven beyond doubt. Care for your body and your mind will be in good condition also.

There have been dietary plans for as long as I can remember. Recent research in the US suggested that, over the longer term, people who embarked on diets ended up three to four pounds heavier than they started. Weight is an attitude of mind. Fatness is an internal belief, based on patterns and beliefs from the past. Body image is created and owned by you. You choose.

On my wall, I have a picture of myself in excellent health, muscled and fit. I see it consciously or unconsciously every day.

It is in front of me now. Create your own image of yourself, fit and in perfect health, using the power of your recall from a past time, or your imagination. Step into that image inside your mind now. See what you will see, hear what you will hear and feel what you will feel as you are inside that image now.

Go forward to a time when you will be that image. Let your unconscious mind decide the most appropriate time. As you are in that future time, step out of the image and see yourself as you will be in that time. Now come back to the now.

Everything you will achieve starts with your health. 'Healthy body, healthy mind'. Eat sensibly. You know the best ideas: eat your biggest meal at the start of the day; the second biggest at lunchtime; the smallest in the evening. Go to bed with a light stomach and sleep well. Eat a balanced diet, including fresh fruit and vegetables. A reasonable amount of protein each day. Pasta, pulses, rice, for energy.

Drink no more than a modest amount of alcohol, spread over the week, rather than one binge. Red wine is good for the heart and digestion. Some has bioflavinoids from the black grape skin. These help prevent cancer.

Most of all, whatever you do, drink six pints of water every day. It flushes the kidneys, cleans and dilutes the bloodstream and is marvellous for the skin. You will look and feel well and think clearly.

Exercise for at least half an hour each day. Just enough to get the blood moving around your body. Make exercise enjoyable, rather than stressful or a chore.

So, for today, work out your chosen dietary and exercise plan. Diarise it, stick to it and reward yourself from time to time as you see and feel the changes that are taking place and hear the compliments from those you care about and whose opinions you value.

Day 2 - Learning to relax

Much has been written and talked about meditation. Transcendental meditation, like the martial arts, seemed to involve many years of practice. I believe you can achieve much the same for yourself in a simpler and quicker way.

The value of meditation is threefold: to release stress; to clear the mind of any negative thoughts or internal dialogue which may have been there before; to open a space for your creative brain to slip original thoughts and ideas into. This is of inestimable value in trading. Inspiration can make the difference between ordinary and superlative performance.

Before proposing the meditation method, think also about dreams. All the great geniuses of time managed their dreams. Einstein dreamed the theory of relativity. Many of the great inventors created their most brilliantly original ideas in dream. Learn how to manage your dreaming process.

You can use the power of your unconscious mind to help you make decisions. It is connected to the universal consciousness. Before you sleep, consider a challenge or question that needs resolution. Put both sides to your unconscious. Entrust the process to your dreaming philosophy and power of analysis.

Keep a notebook beside you whenever you dream or meditate. Make notes of what you have dreamt immediately you wake, or come out of the meditative state. Notice over time, how much, more you can recall.

For today, plan how you will fit meditation into your daily routine. First thing in the morning or early evening is good. You can create the space to meditate any time you choose. Allocate time to your days.

Find a quiet place where you will not be disturbed for up to half an hour. Sit upright in a comfortable, well-supporting chair, or lie flat in bed, preferably without a pillow. Rest your hands, palms down. Relax your body from the toes and feet upwards. Focus on each part in turn. Think of the sound of waves on a beach, gently flowing, as you progressively relax.

Clear your mind in any way that works for you. When I started, I used to think about a blank, white wall. At first, the internal dialogue chattered away, or music came into my mind. I blanked it out again. On the occasions that did not work, I simply said 'be quiet', in a commanding tone, inside my mind.

Be patient. Over time, your meditation will become calmer, longer and deeper. When you choose to wake, come out of your state gently and slowly, bringing positive, stimulating thoughts about the day into your mind. Notice and note all the positive changes you are making in every aspect of your life.

Day 3 - Sensory acuity and peripheral vision

There are 10,000,000,000[11] nerve cells in your mind/body. Your awareness extends well beyond your physical body. We have forgotten more senses than we know we have. We are connected to a limitless universe of possibilities. We have aspects of awareness which are underused and yet are available to us every moment of every day. We can use much more of our sensory acuity.

There are many ways to access this. Meditation is one. The best learning and understanding state is when the conscious and unconscious mind are in harmony, seeing and feeling things together, now.

Here is another way. Pick a spot, or small feature of the room in front of you, above head height and at least three metres away. Focus all your attention on it. As you become more focused, let your awareness spread out at each side of you, all the while remaining looking at the distant object. Become aware now that you are seeing things either side of you and even behind the line of your eyes. Relax and let what happens happen. You are now using your peripheral vision.

This can also achieve the trance or learning state. Remain in this state as long as you wish. Quiet any negative or unproductive internal dialogue and become aware of creative or useful thoughts that pop into your mind from your unconscious.

Start today and as you become more peripherally aware, understand that you can use this state in any trading situation, especially when you wish to achieve calmness, or clear your mind for optimal thinking or original and creative ideas. Maybe when you have a choice to make or an issue to resolve. Trust your unconscious mind. It is connected to the limitless potential of the universe.

Day 4 - Understanding representation systems and sub-modalities

Each of us has a unique pattern of representation systems. By this I mean the means by which the mind represents an internal real or imaginary experience of the world. What is happening inside you right now, as you read these words - pictures, feelings, sounds, smells, tastes, any or all?

Become aware of how your mind receives and processes information best. Do you learn and understand best from pictures, feelings, hearing something, reading or collecting information and analysing it. Find out which pattern works best for you. Understand what works best for other people. You could choose to communicate with them in the medium that works for them. Or you could remain as you are. It is your choice.

In my experience, how someone expresses themselves, may not give the real clue to how they process information best. Some people are different. I produce a lot of verbal output, and I learn best through seeing and doing something.

The three major senses are: visual; auditory; and kinaesthetic. You may use any or all of these. As part of your adaptability and flexibility, try them all. For some people, the information in the markets is better in pictures (e.g. graphs), than numbers.

Each of the 'representation systems' can be further subdivided into 'submodalities' - component parts. So, pictures can be divided into colours, focus, nearness, frame size, movement, etc.

For today, understand your own optimal pattern of rep systems. With their permission, understand your partner's or a friend's. Practice using different patterns. Notice how you need no longer 'talk at cross purposes'. One tip: everyone can make pictures. By and large, women are more visual as a group. Use the magic of language to paint pictures in peoples' minds - and your own.

Analyse your own internal representations into their submodalities. Compare a positive with a negative memory. Notice which submodality(ies) appear most important in each. Find the one(s) that drive the internal representation. Take the driver for positive internal images and enhance that submodality in any negative representations. Play with the control of this driver. If it is nearness, try moving the negative picture nearer or further away. What happens?

Understand how much more power you are already having over your internal and external experiences and relationships.

Day 5 - Setting your Mission

What is your mission in life? Step outside of yourself and look at yourself and your life. Go forward to the end of your life. Look back with your own eyes and ask yourself "what have I achieved in my life that made a significant difference, or that people can remember me by.

Here's an example. My mission is to create an environment in which peoples' natural talents can flourish.

What is your mission in trading? In how many ways does this fit with your overall mission in life? Have a mission, which is a clear, enduring, guiding light or beacon in your life...something you feel can be very much part of you...when you say it to yourself, it sounds right. Create an internal representation that seems to capture your mission in trading. Take it out into the future, to the end of that time, now. Let your unconscious mind decide. Leave it out there and come back to the now. Write it down and look at it every day.

Day 6 - Determining your values

What are your values in trading? For what purposes for yourself do you trade?

For today, ask yourself why trading is important for you? Keep asking yourself the question, over and over. Write down whatever comes into mind. You may have five or six values or more, which emerge. Some might include financial gain, others success, yet others fulfilment or respect, etc. What is really, really important for you, and you alone?

Refine your list. Reflect on those values. What do you feel about them? Listen for whether they appear to be driven away from a negative place or towards a positive outcome.

Day 7 - Understanding your beliefs

What are your core beliefs, for yourself, about trading? What are your beliefs about yourself as a trader? How do you believe now that you are successful? Go out into the future, to a time when you have been successful and what do you feel are the positives as you are feeling good about that now?

Write down your positive and enhancing beliefs. Look at them. For each, write down at least three ways in which that belief can make you the trader you plan to become now. If you wish, make an internal representation of each belief. Take it forward to a time where it seems most appropriate to be in relation to the growing success of your trading. Step outside the belief in your mind and leave it in that future space. Come back to the now.

Day 8 - Removing a limiting decision or belief

For some, the odd negative or limiting belief may have popped in. Change those now at your choice.

Just go inside now and get a sense or a feeling of where any negative belief may have come from. Become aware of the person from your childhood who may have represented that belief or otherwise presented it to you. It was never your belief, it was always their belief and you took it on at that time when you were young, because it was in your awareness at the time and in some way it may have seemed right.

Sometime, it became a limitation. Its purpose was to carry forward a positive learning that was there for you. You no longer need it.

Close your eyes and create a representation, which is right for you, of that belief. Make it no bigger than a box you could carry. Now, inside yourself, use the limitless power of your imagination to create vividly beautiful wrapping paper, ribbons and whatever. Wrap the representation with all your loving care, in the beautiful paper.

In your mind, give the beautiful wrapped present to the person from whom the belief came originally, with all your love and tender care. It was never your belief, it was theirs. Indeed, it may not have been theirs originally, it may have come from their past...So give that belief back right now, as you no longer need it, now you have stored the positive learnings in that special place.

Day 9 - Understanding your filters

Take the time to complete the following simple questionnaire. Let your unconscious mind intuitively or logically represent the answers and the interpretations. Understanding the key filters through which you process all experience, you could choose to change them or share them with someone special so that they understand you even better. Use that understanding to enhance your growing success.

Try on the other values, which do not currently represent you, just to see how the rest of the world feels. What are the messages that come to you inside about the new vista of opportunities opening before you?

Question **What do you want from your trading?**
Filter   Towards/away from
Question **Why are you choosing to do what you do?**
Filter   Possibility/necessity
Question **How do you know when you've traded well?**
Filter   Internal/external evidence
Question **How do you know other traders are good?**
Filter   See/hear/do/read
Question **How often do they have to do that to convince you?**
Filter   Automatic/x times/always
Question **In a new situation do you act or reflect first?**
Filter   Active/reflective/both
Question **Describe a time when you were happiest trading?**
Filter   Things/people/systems
Question **Describe your favourite restaurant.**
Filter   People/places/things

If we worked together at trading, would you want the details or the big picture first?

Specific/global

When you come to trading fresh, what is different from the last time you were trading?

Same/different/exception

Describe a trading situation that troubled you?

Associated/disassociated

(In associated you see the memory through your own eyes).

Through the above, you have elicited and understood your primary filters. Try in vain to stop thinking about the many ways this understanding is helping you.

Day 10 - Setting your goals

Sit down now, with two pieces of paper. On the first, write down your long-term goals from trading. What you will achieve for yourself. Now, on the second, write the goals you will have for the next year.

For each goal, make an internal picture and, as before, put it out into your future.

Day 11 - Visualising your outcome

Take an outcome, which for you seems to most powerfully represent your most important goal from yesterday. One which, in achieving it, you will realise how much you have changed. Now, make sure it is only for you (although others may benefit through you), that it is ethical, decent and generally sound.

Create a representation for yourself as if you have that outcome now. What is the last thing that needs to happen for you to know that you have that outcome? That's right. See it through your own eyes. Now, take that outcome to a future time in which your unconscious mind suggests it is most appropriate to be set. Step out of the picture and entrust the outcome to your unconscious mind at the time that is right. Come back to the now

Use this as many time sand as often as you wish.

Day 12 - Determining your trading plan

In how many ways you are already realising the power of your unconscious mind. And as your conscious mind becomes aware of the ways in which you are changing now, use the partnership of your conscious and unconscious mind to create a trading plan that looks and feels right for you.

The elements are: the medium and longer-term goals; the strategy you will use to achieve these; the resources you will need to implement the strategy. In addition, you will have decided your own trading style and the methods and techniques from which you will draw your actions, knowing that this 30 day program is already framing your mentality, style, attitude, beliefs and positive states.

Write down all these things and the practical steps you will take to implement your trading plan, understanding that, as you write it on paper, you are writing it into your unconscious mind also. The mind that never forgets anything and from which you can recall as you choose.

Write down and review the measures you will use to determine and observe your growing success now.

Schedule a time, at the end or beginning of any trading day or week, when you will review your progress and performance for that period and overall, so that you are learning and growing every day. Use these questions and any other question, which by asking it of yourself means that you recognise your growing and changing:

- What specifically have I done well?
- Where can I continue to improve?
- Overall, how well am I doing?

Day 13 - Learning how to learn

How did you learn how to drive? How did you learn how to ride a bicycle, or even to walk? How did you learn to read, write, or even speak?

By now, you will be having many insights.

When you were born, you weren't even thinking about riding a bike. You were *unconsciously incompetent* to ride a bike. When you first sat on a bike, with the intention to learn to ride, what were the thoughts flooding your mind. Distilling them, you may have realised *consciously* that you were *incompetent* yet to ride a bike.

After many attempts you were able to ride without falling off or anyone holding the seat. You may have been a little wobbly or uncertain, but you had made it. You were *consciously competent* to ride a bike.

Later, you were very much more confident, so that you could leap on the bike and ride off with your friends, without so much as a thought of whether you might fall off. You had become *unconsciously competent* to ride a bike.

This is the process we go through in acquiring any skill. You may be very aware now of the many ways in which you are seeing change and opportunity in your trading. You may be realising that you have reached conscious competence as you have tried and practised these skills and techniques. You may even have noticed that you, or other people, were already doing these things, out of conscious awareness. Now that you understand, so many choices to improve still further.

Take some time to choose and practise the areas of competence, which seem right for you, to practise until they have been reinstalled now.

We learn best in trance. Meditation is a good way. Going out into a peripheral state can enhance learning. You may be seeing or feeling many other ways or times in which you know you are in trance. Rapture, ecstasy and even boredom are trance states. As you go deeper, reading this book, you are understanding and learning so much now...didn't you?

So, someone mentions memory. "I have a hopeless memory" (limiting belief). The unconscious mind records and remembers everything. Dreaming is a process for analysing, sorting, connecting, deleting...What you need is recall. Here's how.

Whenever you wish to learn something, make a picture. Look up and to your left as you do this (this stores the memory in visual recall). Associate into the picture anything, which seems to you to be appropriate. This works very well for remembering peoples' names. Now, when you want to recall a memory, look up and to the left and see what pops in...

Day 14 - Understanding how to be your best

What

- Realise your limitless potential in trading, as in life.
- Understand all the things you are already doing, often unconsciously.
- Learn how to learn - best.
- Learn how to be your best in any trading situation.

How and Why

- Model excellence - create lasting success.
- Choose your trading goals.
- Visualise the outcomes.
- Set your anchors.
- Be in rapport.
- STOP...or change your internal dialogue.
- See, hear, do and have fun trading.
- So that you have more choices.

Where and When

- In every aspect of your life and trading.
- Whenever you choose...for yourself.

Day 15 - Achieving self-mastery

Use all these things to better understand yourself.

- Review Rotella's 13 characteristics. Try them on.
- Listen more, talk less.
- Reflect on how your intelligence and your emotions can work positively in harmony.

- Become open to your internal feelings.
- Be aware of the effects on your behaviours and the attitudes of those around you.
- Put yourself at cause in everything - yes, everything you do. Life is a series of choices

Day 16 - Understanding and improving your strategies

- Work with a partner to understand the structure of your strategies.
- What is going on inside you as you run them?
- What is happening inside you and in your language as you run your motivation strategy? (The strategy that gets you up for doing something).
- Do the same for:
  - your decision strategy (how you decide);
  - your convincer strategy;
  - your reassurance strategy.

Now, as you review these, what do you observe? Where can you make these even more productive and resourceful? For example, see what happens when you introduce a question like "is this right for me?" or "do I really want to do this?" or "does this fit with my plan or strategy?" before you really go for it. If it still feels right, do it.

For any strategy improvement, check the original strategy, make the change, check for the desired effect, if it is not there, go back and review/modify, otherwise exit.

This strategy review and improvement process can be used for anything in your life - trading, learning, loving...

Day 17 - Making the most of your capabilities

- Take a sheet of A4 paper. Divide it into quarters.
- Head up the first box 'What do I enjoy doing?'

- Head up the second box 'What am I good at?'
- Head up the third box 'What makes money?'
- Head up the fourth box 'What fits with my mission?'

Now, without editing, fill in each box.

When you have finished, cross out everything, which is not in all four boxes.

You will be left with a list of only those things, which fit with your mission, you enjoy doing, you are good at and can earn you money. Why would you want to do anything else? Open your mind for one more moment and see if there isn't anything else you feel would sound right in all four lists?

Life is a series of choices - for you.

Day 18 - Creating positive internal dialogue

Do you have a voice inside you that speaks to you from time to time? Many people do. This is internal dialogue. Has this voice, or any other voice inside you, ever told you off, admonished, chastised or criticised you in any way, at any time?

If it has, why don't you STOP ... right now.

Think of someone who you know loves you, or appreciates you and the positives about you. It could be someone from your present, or your past. It could even be a dream lover, who will love you without condition, as you are and for what you are.

Imagine or recall the way that they speak to you, with love or appreciation...

Why would you want to speak to yourself any other way?

Stephen Covey suggests that you repeat the affirmation "I like myself, I like myself..." every day. Louise Hay recommends that you look at yourself in the mirror, at least once a day and say to yourself "I love myself and everything about me".

After I had been ill, I noticed that my self-talk was full of imperatives: "I must do this...I've got to do that...I should have done that...I ought to do this...etc."

I decided there and then to eliminate the imperatives from my self-talk. Life is a series of choices: "I can do this...I could do that...I would like to do this...I want to do that...I'm going to do this...I am able to do that...etc."

As you try these ideas on, you may already be noticing the changes and the new possibilities opening up before you...

Day 19 - Deciding with conviction - matching life and trading values

On Day 6, you determined your core values for trading.

Today, take a sheet of paper and write the following headings, evenly spaced:

- Career/Business/Professional
- Relationships and Social
- Home and Family
- Leisure
- Health and Fitness
- Spiritual

For each of these values and using the same methodology as before, quickly write down the four to eight most important things to you. Keep going and capture the spontaneous thoughts, as they occur.

Now look at each of these values and those you elicited earlier for trading. Find the three, which seem to be most in common across all lists and which also appear in the trading values list. Denote them as A, B and C.

Ask yourself the following questions in order:

Would I need B in order to have A; would I need C in order to have A; would I need C in order to have B?

From these questions, you will be able to determine the order of importance of these values, which are common to your life as well as your trading. Sleep on these and let your unconscious mind go to work overnight.

Day 20 - Deciding with Conviction - living your trading values

As early as possible on the following day, repeat the latter part of the above exercise.

Now you can be confident you have your core values in both life and trading, do the following:

In your own time, place and space, mark out three positions on the floor, perhaps with three blank sheets of paper. Put them no more than a pace apart, wherever seems or feels right for you.

Sitting comfortably in a chair, take the most important value, or the first that comes to mind. Think of a time when you know this value was present in what you were doing, feeling or being. Be in that time now and see, hear and feel what you were experiencing at that time. Use the power of submodalities to really be in that moment.

Do the same for each of the other two values. Find a way to break the state, by doing or thinking something banal, or imagine a blank screen in your mind.

Now, repeat the process of returning to that time where you were in your first value. Fill yourself up with the experience and, when it is at its height or the strongest, step onto the first sheet of paper.

Keep hold of the feelings and images inside you and think of the time when you experienced your second value. When you are filled up, step onto the second sheet of paper.

Repeat the process for your third value, while keeping hold of the feelings from your second value. Step onto the third sheet of paper.

Break the state and step away from the sheets of paper. When you are ready, repeat the process, stepping through your core values.

Do this as many times as you wish until the experience of associating into your values becomes automatic.

Now, wherever, or whenever you are, you can imagine your three pieces of paper on the floor ahead of you and walk through your core values.

So now, think of a time when you needed to be at your best, trading. As you think of that time now, walk through your core values and notice the changes you may already be experiencing. Maybe you are seeing things in a new light now, feeling more focused, speaking positively to yourself inside.

Finally, plan or review a trading decision you wish to make. Fill your mind with the factors to consider and then walk through your values, knowing that the answer that pops into your mind is right for you.

Now you can decide with the conviction of your core values, go forward to a real or imagined time in the future, when you are making an important decision. As you see, hear or feel yourself, step into that picture and having walked through your values, did you notice the changes you are experiencing now?

Day 21 - Creating rapport (1) - eye cues

Today and tomorrow is about choice in creating rapport with the people around you.

When there is calmness in your personal life and you can choose to be at ease with yourself in any aspect, then you can be at your best, creating rapport with anyone, at ease, including yourself... You could also use these techniques in order to break rapport or create negative rapport, so that you can disengage, consciously or unconsciously, being able to be yourself in any way that seems right for you.

We'll start with eye cues. Some people are oppositely organised (that is, their eye patterns will work in the opposite way to the following), and it is easiest to assume that almost everyone is 'normally' organised.

Ask someone an open question (one for which the answer is more than just a single word, such as yes or no). As they answer, watch their eyes. The eyes are connected to the various parts of the brain.

Movement up and to the left as you look at them indicates they are making a picture inside. Up and to the right means they are recalling a picture that they have previously seen outside or inside themselves.

Movement across left, denotes creating sounds inside and across right is recalling sounds.

Down to the left as you look at their face, indicates they are accessing their feelings, or may be about to use a 'physical' predicate or description. Down to the right, is where self-talk, data, facts, criteria, etc are accessed.

Have fun trying these and please be aware of other peoples' wishes or feelings. If you make what you are doing obvious, or start telling people what they are doing, you may upset, annoy or otherwise unsettle the person. The skills you are using are to privately enhance the basis and quality of your understanding and relationships. If you start playing these things, or the following section back to them, they may feel they are being 'analysed'.

Listen all the while to their language. Remember the section on representations that we covered earlier. You could choose the information you are discovering to help create superb rapport.

I dislike the 'self-confession' shows, such as Jerry Springer, but they are great for practising my understanding of eye cues. Watching Blind Date and the Clinton tapes was most enlightening also.

Day 22 - Creating rapport (2) - mirroring and matching

Remember, 55% of communication is non-verbal. Babies cannot see much more than a foot when they are born. For some time, they make out shapes and movements in their immediate vicinity. What do they see most of, other than the face and eyes of the person holding them?

As they grow older, they spend a lot of time sitting and watching. They learn so much from what they observe, unconsciously matching it with the sounds that they hear. We all learned the skills I am teaching you here, at an early age. The process was 'hit and miss' however. I am now offering you the chance to 'unpack' these skills, review them, improve them, practise and reinstall them to enhance any aspect of your life you choose.

As you are standing or sitting, communicating with someone (which of course you can also do unconsciously), you may be aware when you are in rapport that your body posture is similar. Did you ever notice that?

Many people since Desmond Morris have written about 'body language'. You may be able to understand so much from someone's posture. And, suppose they sighed, or breathed in a certain way...

What you will learn and practise today, I ask you to do subtly and with respect for someone else's model of the world. We are not talking of mimicry. That is what children do, with voice or posture. You may have found that irritating.

When you use the following skills subtly, you can improve the quality of any relationship. Since Dale Carnegie first wrote 'How to Win Friends and Influence People', it has been acceptable to use and improve your skills in the quality of your business and personal relationships.

As you sit or stand with someone, you may notice their body posture, breathing, tonality, facial expressions, hand movements and even phrases or other mannerisms they use. As you begin to quietly and carefully match these, you may find yourself being or feeling in rapport. You can match their whole posture, or just part of it. For example, if you are sat across a desk or table, you could match just the upper body.

People often ask me whether others spot this happening. If they do, you have an opportunity to practise and improve further. No one has ever drawn my attention to what I was doing, unless I first asked them to take part in an exercise.

Think of all the situations in which you will be able to use all these new skills and, having used them in your trading or any aspect of your life, how many new possibilities are opening up.

Now you can be your best self, at ease with anyone, including yourself, at any time, then in how many ways will your whole trading experience have improved, by the time you have realised that already?

Day 23 - Managing perceptual positions

Now you have accumulated so many skills that you can have an understanding in your conscious, or your unconscious, mind. Being able to see the world from someone else" perspective, or even to be the proverbial 'fly on the wall' can dramatically the possibilities in trading.

In how many ways does your trading change and improve when you can step outside yourself and see the situation from someone else's perspective, or especially an impartial position?

How well can you model the skills of another when you can 'be in their shoes' whenever you wish.

Find a quiet space, maybe in meditation, or elsewhere. Fill yourself with an awareness of what you are seeing, hearing and feeling inside yourself. Using all the skills of submodalities and others, enrich your experience of what is happening inside yourself now, knowing you can always do this at will. You are now deep in position 1.

Choose a friend who enjoys having fun. Go into an open space together. Have the friend walk along, thinking of a very specific situation, maybe something they imagine themselves going to. Walk one pace behind them, opening your mind, so that the spontaneous thoughts and feelings can emerge and grow in your unconscious mind. Allow your unconscious awareness to flow into that of the friend ahead of you, as you are walking 'in their shoes'.

After a minute or two, stop and tell them what you sensed or felt was in their mind.

Notice how your perception grows as you practise this exercise. You could also do this as you talk with someone else. Have an impression of leaving your own position and going into theirs. How different do things seem now. You are in position 2.

Recall or be in a time as you are listening to, or engaging with someone else. Or, do the same for a trading situation. Now step outside yourself and move your awareness up onto the ceiling, or to some other place where you can have a completely detached view, sense or feeling of what is happening. This is position 3.

Practise these positions every day until they become unconscious. If ever you wish to review a trading situation or decision, do it from all three positions. Use this ability in your relationships and see yourself from positions 2 and 3, as you choose.

Day 24 - Listening, well

I learned from my father the ability to talk...too much. A basic shyness in personality led to my deciding to engage more with people verbally. Unfortunately, lack of self-esteem also meant that I was seeking to be accepted and, as well as talking too much, I had become practised in trying to impose my view on others...

I am learning, changing and growing. I love that capacity of 'gravitas', being able to be cool and detached as appropriate before offering the appropriate thought at just the right moment.

As a mentor, coach and therapist, it is ideal that one listens well to another. The good counsellor listens, plays back accurately, acknowledges appropriately and facilitates the environment where

Understand Derivatives in a Day

Financial derivatives are used as highly-geared vehicles for making money, saving money or preventing its loss. They also have the ability to exploit volatility, guarantee results and avoid taxes. But only if they are used correctly.

Learn...How private investors get started... To Hedge, Straddle and control Risk... Ways to limit the downside but not the upside... About risk free derivative strategies... Trading Psychology - Fear, Hope and Greed... Also, the History of Derivatives; Currency Speculation; Long and Short puts; Tarantula Trading; and much more.

112 pages   ISBN:1-873668-56-2   £6.95

Understand Financial Risk in a Day

Risk management is all about minimising risks and maximising opportunities. Those who understand what they should be doing, as a result of their risk calculations, will usually come out as winners.

Understand Financial Risk in a Day is a perfect introduction to the subject. Light on detailed formulae and heavy on easy-to-follow examples it will lead the reader to a greater awareness of how to evaluate the risks they are facing and adapt a strategy to create the best possible outcome.

96 pages   ISBN:1-873668-24-4   £6.95

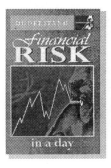

Understand Swaps in a Day

The last twenty years have seen the largest upheaval of the financial sector in history. This turbulence has been induced by an unparalleled growth in the use of derivatives, and Swaps in particular. These days everyone is doing it. Swaps and Swap bi-products are being used by all financial institutions, major quoted companies and governments around the world. This book offers a practical introduction to the subject for those with little or no knowledge of the Swap markets.

128 pages   ISBN:1-873668-74-0   £6.95

Investing in Options: For the Private Investor

A hardback book which shows you exactly how to 'gear' your money to provide more growth. Step-by-step it teaches how you appraise an options position, looking at the rewards and risks, and then how to execute a deal. There are plenty of examples to show you exactly how its done and how to trade profitably.

For the experienced options buyer there are examples of option combinations which can be used to create almost any desired outcome. With options you can make money whichever direction the market is moving.

128 pages   1-873668-39-2   £14.95   Hardback

Investing for the Long Term

This book is aimed at those savvy investors who are content to ride out short term fluctuations in the markets in order to realise bigger long term gains. Be it for school fees, a larger house or retirement, if you need money in more than 10 years time, this book is for you. Very comprehensive; covering everything from growth versus income to understanding company accounts, and from downturns, corrections & crashes to looking at the larger economic picture.

192 pages   1-873668-76-7   £14.95   Hardback

Successful Spread betting

Spread Betting offers investors a simple and direct way of dealing in the world's financial markets and has significant advantages over other methods of dealing: ...It gives you access to financial markets in which you couldn't normally deal without being a registered broker, for example foreign exchange ...Any money you make from Spread Betting is Tax Free ...You can also bet on events and outcomes in the sporting world ...There are no dealing charges - no brokerage or commission fees ...Spread Betting firms offer instant dealing and extended hours so you can take out a position even when the underlying markets are closed.

160 pages   ISBN:1-873668-58-9   £12.95

Investing on the Internet

The Internet is revolutionising the way ordinary investors are going about increasing their personal wealth. For the first time everyone can now access information that used to be available only to the investment professionals. And with *Investing on the Internet*, you can be at the forefront of this transformation.

This handy guide will lead you to the best investment tools there are on the web, almost all of which are completely free. Full site addresses are given with a review of content, speed and usefulness.

192 pages   ISBN:1-873668-73-2   £4.95

International Dictionary of Personal Finance

This dictionary provides a basic vocabulary of terms used in the world of personal finance, from 'A' shares to zero-rating and from accelerated depreciation to yield. Words used in all areas of finance are covered, not just those from basic investment, but also from the arenas of banking, law, national insurance and tax. Both British and American usages are included.

128 pages   ISBN:1-873668-54-6   £6.95

International Dictionary of Derivatives

A dictionary of terms designed to aid all those involved, or about to become involved, with these complex financial instruments. Nothing is missed out, with explanations and diagrams from Accrual Options and Agrigation through to ZEPOs and Zero Gain Collars. Also contains a list of acronyms.

96 pages   ISBN:1-873668-57-0   £6.95

Timing the Financial Markets:
Charting your way to profit

Shows all levels of investors how to construct charts and graphs of price movements for bonds, shares and commodities. Then it explains, in easy-to-understand language, how to interpret the results and turn them into profit. With computers taking over so much of the trading activity on the world's stockmarkets (news programmes call it "automated trading"), charting is becoming a more and more powerful technique.

96 pages   ISBN:1-873668-47-3   £6.95

Book Ordering

To order any of these books, please order on the world wide web at **www.takethat.co.uk** or complete the form below or use a plain piece of paper and send to:

Europe/Asia
TTL, PO Box 200, Harrogate HG1 2YR, England (or fax to 01423-526035, or email: sales@net-works.co.uk).

USA/Canada
Trafalgar Square, PO Box 257, Howe Hill Road, North Pomfret, Vermont 05053 (or fax to 802-457-1913, call toll free 800-423-4525, or email: tsquare@sover.net)

Postage and handling charge:
UK - £1 for first book, and 50p for each additional book
USA - $5 for first book, and $2 for each additional book (all shipments by UPS, please provide street address).
Elsewhere - £3 for first book, and £1.50 for each additional book via surface post (for airmail and courier rates, please fax or email for a price quote)

Book	Qty	Price

☐ I enclose payment for _____

Postage

Total:

☐ Please debit my Visa/Amex/Mastercard No:

Expiry date: [ ][ ][ ][ ]   Signature: _____

Name: _____

Address: _____

_____

_____

Postcode/Zip: _____

nlp